Along the
Rio Grande

Monsignor Henry Granjon, Bishop of the Diocese of Tucson. (Courtesy Archives of the Diocese of Tucson, Arizona.)

Along the Rio Grande

A Pastoral Visit
to Southwest New Mexico
in 1902

*Monsignor Henry Granjon,
Bishop of Tucson*

Edited and Annotated by Michael Romero Taylor
Translated by Mary W. de López

Illustrations by Anthony Pennock

Published in cooperation with the
Historical Society of New Mexico

University of New Mexico Press
Albuquerque

Library of Congress Cataloging-in-Publication Data
Granjon, Henry, 1863–1922.
Along the Rio Grande.

  Bibliography: p.
  Includes index.
  1. New Mexico—Social life and customs. 2. New Mexico—Religious life and customs. 3. New Mexico—Description and travel. 4. Granjon, Henry, 1863–1922—Journeys—New Mexico. 5. Visitations, Ecclesiastical—New Mexico. I. Taylor, Michael Romero. II. Historical Society of New Mexico. III. Title.
F801.C915   1986   917.89′6044   86-11390
ISBN 0-8263-0903-8
ISBN 0-8263-0904-6 (pbk.)

© 1986 by the University of New Mexico Press.
All rights reserved.
First edition.

Dedicated to the wonderful people
within the newly created Diocese of Las Cruces
of whose parents and grandparents
Bishop Granjon writes so affectionately.

Contents

Illustrations	ix
Foreword	xi
Acknowledgments	xiii

1. Introduction — 3
2. Along the Rio Grande — 15
   A little-known land / 17
   Story of camels / 26
   Continuation of trip by train / 32
   Solemn reception / 36
   Dean of Arizona missionaries / 41
   "In terra deserta" / 49
   Towns of Arizona / 56
   The evening of a beautiful day / 63
   San Miguel / 79
   Confirmation at La Mesa / 84
   The feast of the Ascension / 90
   Confirmation at Chamberino / 95
   El Paso / 104
   Departure from Tularosa and arrival at Alamogordo / 109
   Tribulations of a traveler in a freight car / 114

Notes	119
Selected Sources	141
Index	145

Illustrations

Map
New Mexico Portion of the Diocese of Tucson / 67

Monsignor Henry Granjon / frontispiece
Bishop Granjon at his desk / 68
A.T.&.S.F. Railway station, Las Cruces / 69
Las Cruces in 1903 / 69
St. Genevieve's Church / 70
Loretto Academy, Las Cruces / 70
San Albino Church, Mesilla / 71
Calle Santiago in Mesilla / 71
Bosque Seco Church / 72
Interior of the Bosque Seco Church / 73
San José Church, La Mesa / 73
Acequia Madre, Las Cruces / 74
Adobe houses in Tularosa / 74
Collecting mesquite in the Mesilla Valley / 75
Jacal in Mesilla / 75
Rural Mesilla / 76
Family in the Mesilla Valley / 76
Early settlement in old "Mesquite Lake" / 77
Thomas J. Bull's vineyard, Mesilla / 77
Las Cruces and the Organ Mountains / 78

Foreword

The Historical Society of New Mexico is pleased to cosponsor *Along the Rio Grande: A Pastoral Visit to Southwest New Mexico in 1902* as the tenth volume in the copublication series the Historical Society has with the University of New Mexico Press. This journal by Monsignor Henry Granjon, bishop of Tucson, is a rich source on the daily life and family customs of ordinary people in southern New Mexico at the turn of the century.

The appointment of Bishop Jean Baptiste Lamy to the Diocese of Santa Fe in the mid-nineteenth century resulted in many French priests eventually coming to serve in the Southwest; Henry Granjon was one. In 1900, after just ten years as a missionary in Arizona, Granjon became the bishop of Tucson, succeeding another Frenchman whom Lamy had selected.

Bishop Granjon's diocese included all of the Arizona Territory and Grant, Luna, Sierra, and Doña Ana counties in New Mexico. To learn more about his parishes in southwest New Mexico, Bishop Granjon toured the Mesilla Valley and surrounding area and administered the sacrament of confirmation in May 1902. The following year a Lyon Missionary Society published in French Bishop Granjon's account of his trip. Missionaries around the world surely recognized in Granjon's journal descriptions of the very struggles they faced in spreading Catholicism: the gains made by Protestants in the mission field and the inroads made by secular and material interests into the lives of the faithful. But the journal is far more than a commentary on religious life; it is in fact an important new source on the social and cultural history of southern New Mexico in the early 1900s.

The original articles published by Bishop Granjon turned up in 1952 in a box of papers uncovered by the family of Michael Romero Taylor when they purchased a building that had served as a rectory in Mesilla. More years passed with the journal and other papers secure in storage, but finally in 1980 a friend of the Taylor family, Mary W. de López, skillfully translated the narrative to preserve the distinctive literary flair of Bishop Granjon. Michael Taylor then thoroughly researched all aspects of the bishop's trip to provide full annotations and an introduction to the journal. The publication of *Along the Rio Grande* fulfills perfectly one of the goals of this copublication series: to make available new primary sources on New Mexico's past.

The officers and directors of the Historical Society for 1986 are: *Officers*—John P. Conron, President; Spencer Wilson, First Vice-President; Charles Bennett, Second Vice-President; John Grasham, Secretary; Joseph W. Stein, Treasurer. *Board*—Thomas E. Chavez, Richard N. Ellis, William F. Gibbs, Austin Hoover, Charlotte Gray Jackson, Myra Ellen Jenkins, Lorraine Lavender, William P. Lock, Michael L. Olsen, Orlando Romero, Albert A. Schroeder, and John P. Wilson.

Acknowledgments

The help and encouragement of the following individuals are greatly appreciated: Thomas Caperton, Margo Charles, Denise Chávez, Tom Chávez, Don Day, Bunny Fontana, Clara Gonzales, Austin Hoover, Trini López, Father Jaime Madrid, Lionel Mestas, Father Mario Potzer, Orlando Romero, Dick Rudisell, Susie Sato, Mary and Paul Taylor, Charlotte Warren, and Leah C. Wright.

The following groups and institutions also provided invaluable assistance: Arizona State University Special Collections, Phoenix; Catholic Archives of Texas, Austin; Catholic University of America, Theology Library, Washington, D.C.; Diocese of El Paso; Diocese of Tucson Archives; New Mexico Historical Society Publications Committee; University of Notre Dame Archives; Rio Grande Historical Collections, New Mexico State University Library, Las Cruces; State Engineers Office, Santa Fe.

Along the Rio Grande

Introduction

Along the Rio Grande is a journal written by the French Bishop Henry Granjon about his southern New Mexico pastoral tour, through the Mesilla Valley and the surrounding area, in 1902. In his journal, the Bishop described the people and the terrain that he encountered as he visited the villages to administer the sacrament of confirmation. Any person who has spent time in the Mesilla Valley will smile knowingly as the good Bishop speaks of the prismatic colors on the Organ Mountains, of shade trees along dusty streets fronted by adobe homes, of glistening fields of chile and alfalfa criss-crossed by numerous *acequias* carrying precious water, of the warmth of the people. While much has changed since Granjon wrote of his travels, the magic of the valley is still very much alive. The Bishop's descriptions of the countryside and its people, as well as his highly opinionated social commentaries, paint a warm, vivid picture of the time and place. Granjon's journal not only provides information on such things as numbers of inhabitants and types of industry, but also gives the reader a feeling of the lives of these southern New Mexicans. Granjon also presents a clear picture of social, economic, and spiritual conditions at the turn of the century.

This journal was originally published in French in 1903 by the Society for the Propagation of Faith in Lyon, France. The Society, which served as the informational clearinghouse for Catholic missionary activities around the world, printed a weekly periodical called *Les Missions Catholiques* that, among other items, contained descriptions of missionary endeavors such as those of Bishop Granjon. The narrative was published in eighteen consecutive issues, from April through August. It was translated into English in its entirety by Mary de López in 1980.[1]

The Mesilla Valley already had a rich and fascinating history at the time of Granjon's visit. For hundreds of years it had been a crossroads through which strangers had passed and where they had encountered the local inhabitants. Long before the Spaniards first ventured up the valley to colonize northern New Mexico in 1598, the Mesilla Valley was a natural trade route for the prehistoric cultures that peopled what we know as northern New Mexico and Mexico. As these prehistoric traders, adventurers, and hunters passed through the valley, they met the local inhabitants living in settlements along terraces and mesas overlooking the river. They left with these people news from afar, religious and social ideas, and new technology. Undoubtedly, some of the travelers were enchanted by the valley and stayed, eventually marrying into the local families.

Generations later, as the Spaniards settled in northern New Mexico during the seventeenth and eighteenth centuries, the Mesilla Valley became an important part of the *Camino Real* (Royal Highway) on the Chihuahua Trail, where the Spaniards stopped at *parajes* (camping spots) to rest, to pasture their livestock, and to fill gourds with water before striking out north across the dreaded ninety-mile stretch of the *Jornada del Muerto* (Journey of the Dead Man). With a sense of awe and a feeling of imminent change, the much reduced indigenous population, whom the Spaniards called "*Mansos,*" watched and heard the creaking of ox carts laden with European clothes, religious articles, crockery, china, and books. Religious, clothed in long robes, and soldiers accompanied the carts; there were also traders, entrepreneurs, and families in search of land driving strange animals—sheep, goats, and cattle—before them.

After the Pueblo Revolt of 1680, the small mission village of El Paso del Norte, which was established before 1659, became a bustling town as a result of the sudden influx of Spanish refugees fleeing the righteous wrath of the northern Pueblo Indians. Along with the Spaniards came Indians from the northern New Mexican village of Isleta del Norte and from the Piro villages in the vicinity of Socorro, New Mexico. These Indians settled in El Paso del Norte (present-day Juárez) and the small villages of Senecú del Sur, Socorro del Sur and Isleta del Sur downriver, and in other newly established villages to the South, also along the river. By the nineteenth century, they had intermarried with remnants of the local *Manso* population, and there also had been an infusion of Spanish blood. These were the people who came up from their villages south of El Paso del Norte in the mid 1800s to settle the villages of Doña Ana, Las Cruces, Mesilla, San Miguel, La Mesa, and, ultimately, Anthony and Tularosa. The majority came as *peones* in search of better farmlands and room to expand.[2] These are the people of whom Granjon speaks so lovingly in his narrative—and they brought change to the valley.

After the War with Mexico and the Gadsden Purchase of 1853, these villagers suddenly found themselves labeled as Americans. They were subject to American laws that few of them could understand, even in Spanish. The new laws governing land ownership were taken advantage of by the Anglos. The valley was soon besieged by an influx of people with a new language, new religions, new sense of business, and new ethics. By the late 1850s, Mesilla and Las Cruces were major links in the complex transportation and trade networks linking the East with the West Coast. With this impetus came fine hotels and restaurants; wholesale stores sprang up serving the intensive mining operations being conducted in the area and supplying military posts with goods which the soldiers were accustomed to having. Some of the Anglos who took advantage of the new opportunities offered in the Mesilla Valley came with the California Column in 1862. This constituted a force of 1,400 Union soldiers who marched from California to New Mexico in order to liberate the Territory from the Confederates, only to find upon their arrival that the Confederates had just retreated from New Mexico back to Texas. Many of the California Column who saw the valley liked it and stayed, marrying into the local families. With the arrival of the railroad in Las Cruces in 1881, the Mesilla Valley saw an even greater number of immigrants and further changes.

This, then, was the cultural milieu into which Bishop Granjon stepped in 1902. He was one of many French priests serving the Southwest at the turn of the century. The first French prelate in the region was Bishop Jean Baptiste Lamy who, by order of the Holy See, was named Bishop of the newly created Diocese of Santa Fe in 1851. The diocese at that time consisted of the Colorado, New Mexico, and Arizona territories, encompassing an area larger than Lamy's native France. Prior to Lamy's appointment, this vast area had been served only by a handful of Mexican priests under the far-away jurisdiction of the Diocese of Durango in Mexico. Lamy managed to swell the ranks of the French clergy in the Southwest by embarking on personal recruiting trips to France and Rome and bringing back missionaries to fill the vast gaps within the huge diocese. However, there were still problems. The French and local clergy did not see eye to eye on a number of issues, such as the new tithing system instituted by Lamy, his use of religious statues from Europe that replaced much of the old folk art, and the forbidden Penitente brotherhood that had helped to maintain an organized system of Catholic faith during the years when ordained clergy were so scarce before the arrival of the French prelates. However, the French brought much-needed schools and hospitals, as well as missionary zeal. Their influence on the region has proven to be of tremendous importance. On September 25, 1868, the Vicarate of Tucson, Arizona was created at the request of Archbishop

Lamy in order to manage the area more effectively. J. B. Salpointe, a Lamy recruit from France, was named Vicar Apostolic.

At the time of Granjon's pastoral tour in 1902, the Diocese of Tucson comprised the Arizona Territory and Grant, Luna, Sierra, and Doña Ana counties in New Mexico. From 1914 until 1982 all of southern New Mexico, from Grant County south, came under the jurisdiction of the Diocese of El Paso. In 1982, the Diocese of Las Cruces was established, comprising the southern one-third of New Mexico, and the Most Reverend Ricardo Espinoza Ramírez was installed as its first bishop.

Bishop Granjon was born on June 13, 1863, the son of a distinguished family in St. Etienne, Loire, France. He received his early education in local schools and part of his college training at Black Rock College in Dublin, Ireland. His unique literary style developed through these years of intensive education. At the age of 19, Granjon entered the priesthood and enrolled in the Suplican Seminaries of Paris and Issy, where he studied philosophy and theology. He was ordained a deacon in December, 1886, and then traveled to Rome for advanced studies at the Angelicum, a Dominican university. At the end of 1887, Granjon was ordained a priest in Lyon and said his first Mass in Brignais, where his family had moved. He continued his studies for three more years, during which time he earned doctorates in philosophy, theology and cannon law. Like many young priests of his time, Granjon yearned to become a missionary. He volunteered to serve the church in Arizona, where he was assigned as assistant pastor to Father Joseph Freri at the Sacred Heart Parish in Tombstone in the fall of 1890. He eventually became pastor at Tombstone, and then was transferred to Prescott in 1896. One year later he received instructions to help with the organization of the American Office of the Society for the Propagation of Faith at St. Mary's Seminary in Baltimore, Maryland. In March 1900, Granjon was appointed Bishop of Tucson, succeeding Bishop Peter Bourgade. On June 17, 1900, at the age of 37, he was consecrated Bishop by Cardinal J. Gibbons in the

Cathedral of Baltimore. Bishop Granjon worked with tremendous missionary zeal to bring the Catholic faith to the vast Diocese of Tucson. In 1914, he was instrumental in establishing the Diocese of El Paso, which consisted of the El Paso area and the counties of southern New Mexico.

Granjon sensed the urgent need to stabilize the beautiful mission church of San Xavier del Bac in southern Arizona. He spent many years and thousands of dollars from his own family fortune to preserve the mission church that stands today as a tribute to the Jesuit missionary zeal and Piman craftsmanship of the seventeenth century.

Henry Granjon died on November 9, 1922 at his family home in France while on a trip to meet with Pope Pius XI. He had served as Bishop of Tucson for 22 years.[3]

Reading this journal gives the reader a good idea of the Bishop's likes and dislikes, his fairness and prejudices. We learn that he had a vivid interest in the local flora, at times calling a particular species by its Latin name and describing in detail the botanical side of the world he saw. Granjon had a gift for describing the terrain and natural surroundings:

> The transparency of the air is so great that, beyond the emptiness of the plaza, one can see, stretching to infinity in the direction of the south for the length of the valley, the high branches of cottonwoods, very distant, lost in the solitude. Over all this sleeping nature hovers a silence of nothingness, immense and unfathomable as that on high, in the depths of the sidereal world.

He remarked continually on the beauty and abundance of the flowers that were brought to the May Devotions of the Blessed Virgin in almost every village that he visited, and that were showered on him in celebration of his visit. And he noted how "the Mexicans are wild about them; they love them no matter where, in old soap boxes, in cracked pots, in the remains of tin cans; they surround them with jealous care. . . ."

Granjon was very much aware of the Spanish heritage, with its strong Moslem influences, that is so evident in the Mesilla Valley. He cited the influence of its language ("the genius of the Castilian tongue lends itself admirably to the expression of delicate and profound feelings"), its architecture ("this is Spain once more, the rural Spain of old, somewhat mixed with Anglo-Saxonism and a relic of Aztec survival"), and its customs. The Bishop had a good sense of humor, as evidenced in his story of the United States Army camels and his lightheartedness in the face of uncomfortable situations, such as the cramped quarters of the churches where he administered the sacrament of confirmation to hundreds of screaming children. Although he had been born into a wealthy family in France, he took the dust, dirt, and simplicity graciously and in stride. His continual allusions to the precious commodity of water are still timely, and, in fact, many of the issues he raised are as controversial now as they were in his day. For example:

> Not a week goes by but that some domain, a patrimony left by ancestors, escapes from its earthly possessors to enlarge the fortune of some industrial entrepreneur of the white race. It is certainly irritating, for whoever has an honest soul and a belief in the eminent justice of things, to see the naive simplicity of this race of children shamefully exploited by the greed of heartless ones . . . and this under the cover of the law.

Granjon was very assertive in pointing out that everything the French did was superb. At the same time, he was critical of the "Anglo Saxon race": "I note with pride this magnificent proof of the incontestable superiority that marks the products of French industry. Assuredly, a head covering [bowler hat] imported from Chicago had not before had such a hard life. Oh, where patriotic vanity lodges itself!" He touched on the camaraderie that existed between the French missionaries, and how they reminisced about their childhood days in France when they ran into one another in the course of their missionary journeys.

The resounding message emphasized by Granjon was the sincere goodness that he felt pervaded the souls of the local mestizos:[4]

> You can ask any service of your *compadre;* it will not be denied. Your house is his, your belongings are at his disposition. . . .
> The home is perhaps only a miserable hut, a *jacal,*[5] there is inside perhaps only a crust of bread, and for sleeping, only an old sheepskin spread on the ground. No matter; all this is yours, the *jacal,* the crust, and the sheepskin.

The quiet but forceful faces of the mestizos described by Granjon embodied a contentment and a sense of belonging still seen today in their grandchildren. This naturalness and sense of family of which Granjon spoke are still woven into the fabric of the valley. The Bishop's concern for mestizo culture and traditions are apparent throughout his journal, in passages such as this:

> Contact with the whites, it is true, tends to make disappear, from day to day, this beautiful urbanity, completely natural and so gracious. The selfish manners of the "invader," as they call the American in their ballads, are not without a disturbing influence on the naturalness which formerly gifted the ancient inhabitants of these regions so well.

Granjon was not subtle in his contempt for what he termed the "white" changes that were occurring throughout his diocese. He used the terms "whites," "Protestants," "Anglo-Saxons," and "Americans" interchangeably. One senses a certain paranoia in Granjon, possibly as a result of the influence that the Protestants had on the Amerian educational system. Granjon felt that this influence was a definite threat to the propagation of the Catholic faith in the Southwest.

Perhaps the Bishop pictured the local mestizo population as a bit too helpless and naive, while he saw the "white race" as a bit too haughty and merciless. As Granjon pointed out, Anglos settled in the valley and brought changes. But so had the Spanish when they came centuries earlier, and the French clergy when they began arriving in northern New Mexico in the 1850s.

Change, then, is not new to the Mesilla Valley—prehistoric Indians brought it, then Spaniards and Mexicans, and, finally, Anglos. The interaction of cultures throughout the years has resulted in a mixture of life styles that is reflected in all aspects of life—family, commerce, farming, architecture, and religion—and that has created a uniquely regional, vibrant spirit still very much in evidence today. That the inhabitants of the Mesilla Valley are very open to change has been pointed out in this historical sketch; but they are also very protective of their heritage. Different ethnic groups have been intermarrying for centuries, and their descendants have been called mestizos, *coyotes*, and Chicanos. Some writers scornfully term them "halfbreeds." What is important to the people, however, is that all are part of the Mesilla Valley, and in this lies their sense of pride and heritage. Recently, within New Mexico, there has been an increased awareness of the heritage of the southern part of the state. The differences between the cultures of southern and northern New Mexico are actually quite remarkable, and the history of this fascinating area is slowly beginning to reveal itself in intriguing tales and surprises. Bishop Henry Granjon's delightful narrative is a candid glimpse of the Mesilla Valley in the early 1900s and a significant addition to the developing story of the area.

Along the Rio Grande

Along the Rio Grande

by
Monsignor Henry Granjon,
Bishop of Tucson
May 1902

It was upon returning from an arduous apostolic tour in that part of the Tucson diocese belonging geographically to the Territory of New Mexico that the following pages were written. The distinguished and learned prelate had as the objective of his trip the stations lining the Rio Grande, from Las Cruces (New Mexico) to El Paso (Texas) on the Mexican border. We will follow him on his interesting and picturesque pilgrimage across regions still little known. This simple account of incidents during the trip, written as the pen flows, will be read with the greatest interest.[6]

I

A little-known land. Immense diocese. A bishop very different from the bishops of Europe. On board the transcontinental railroad. A reformer.[7]

Tucson? Arizona? Who has ever heard mention of it? Where is it found on the world's map? Some time ago, I had occasion to write to an eminent person in Belgium. His answer was slow in coming. I was going to give up waiting for it, when a mutual friend informed me that my correspondent, incredulous, had at first doubted the existence of Arizona and its bishop; then on second thought, he had gone to seek information about them. The long-awaited letter from him finally arrived, attesting to his acquisition of a new geographic notion. How true it is that we grow old learning something every day.

So Arizona exists, indeed. On the map of North America, you will find it in the southwest region of the United States, 33 degrees North in latitude and 113 degrees West in longitude, bordered on the North by Utah, on the East by New Mexico, on the South by Mexico, and on the West by California. Its area is 293,000 square kilometers. This gives it, together with that part of New Mexico included in the Tucson diocese, a total surface area of 310,000 square kilometers, or almost two-thirds of France.

What an immense diocese, you will say. Yes, immense in area, but small in population. It contains only 125,000 souls. A fourth, more or less, are Catholic.

Twenty-five missionaries share the conquest of these vast regions, and serve forty-nine missions furnished with chapels and around one hundred stations without chapels, dispersed through all parts of the Territory, sometimes at enormous distances from one another.

The bishop shares their work, and since he does not have at his side either supernumeraries or the venerable body of canons, that *illustrissima adstantium corona* that surrounds the throne of our bishops in Europe, he himself is his own vicar-general, his own chancellor, his own personal and general secretary, and often his own sexton and altar-boy, not to mention other responsibilities.[8] In this land of democracy carried to the extreme, the head that is adorned by the miter of the church and the hand that holds the cross appear at other hours coiffed by a Mexican *sombrero*, in the case of the former, or, in that of the latter, armed with a gardening tool, a jointing plane, or a trowel . . . unless, having to travel, His Grace heads for the stable to harness up his old horse and take up the "relatively simple reins of government" of its modest harness.[9] At this no one takes offense.

Sweet land, isn't it? One must distinguish: as with many things, there both a good and a bad side to this way of life. But it remains true, given the local customs, that the grave and unpleasant consequences which similar breaches of etiquette would bring elsewhere do not exist here in this new, primitive land, which pushes to the limit the principle of "levelling."

In a society stuffed with egalitarian doctrines, it would be futile and awkward to try to insist on social distinctions and prerogatives of rank. Here the "self-determined people" are determinedly touchy in this regard. In England, when addressing a bishop one says My Lord; here it is simply Sir or Monsieur. Friends and acquaintances who are taking pains to be polite accost you by saying, "How do you do, Bishop?" Any other formula, in their eyes, would reek of servility.

Six weeks ago, on a beautiful morning, let's say in spring, even though there are only two seasons in Arizona, winter and summer, I armed myself with my suitcase, walked to the Tucson railroad station, and "boarded" the Grand Express which connects New Orleans to San Francisco, the Gulf of Mexico to the Pacific Coast.

The expression "boarded," universally used, is very accurate. It is indeed a "crossing" that you will make. The distance traveled between the two cities named above is nearly 4,000 kilometers. The trip lasts four days. A sleeping car is assigned to you, naturally somewhat narrow and rather poorly aired, but very clean. When evening comes, you lie down gratefully, crumbling with fatigue, and are rocked by the wheels of the immense wagon.

In place of the liquid plains of the ocean, it is the unending plains, barren and dry, of the great American Southwest that your giant locomotive will break through with its stempost, for the locomotive has a prow made to cut through the resistance not of salty waves, but of cattle and horses strayed onto the tracks. Most of the time the monotony is the same as it is at sea. To the right, to the left, lonely, endless distances tire the gaze. Above your head is an immense blue hemisphere seared during the long hours of the day by a burning sun.

The first day is the most tiring, and to complete the resemblance to a sea crossing, there are those of weak constitution who do not fail to experience a queasiness just like seasickness. Then the body adjusts. One counts the days, then the hours, that one must remain on board.

The best moments of the crossing are the mornings, when, rested by a regenerating sleep and restored by a box lunch, the passengers feel gay, in a loquacious humor, and renew conversations broken off the night before. Conversations then are continued at great length for which the night, bringing counsel, has furnished new arguments.

I cannot recall without smiling the conversation I had one day under such circumstances with a fine American from Chicago, most recently residing in Arizona, who, not having been duly introduced by a third party in the American way, which would have acquainted him with my qualifications and titles, was completely ignorant of who I was. This good Yankee, recognizing by my own Roman collar a member of the Catholic clergy, had come amiably to sit at my side. When greetings had been exchanged, he next initiated conversation along religious lines, asking me which district I served. I told him that my residence was in Tucson.

"Ah! You reside in Tucson! Do you know the Bishop?"

"Perfectly," I answered without a smile.

"Well, now! Tell me, what kind of a man is he? Is he American?"

"No, he's French."

"Ah, you see, I have an idea—a conviction, a theory—of my own. The day will come—remember this well—when with all the bishops of the United States being American, a profound change will take place in the bosom of the Catholic Church. I myself am Catholic, and I speak to you knowledgeably. On that day the American episcopate, meeting in a solemn session, filled with the immense power of this country and impatient with any foreign meddling, will decree absolute autonomy in religious matters as well as all others. We will have an American pope, an American Catholic church. . . ."

"Permit me," I interjected. "Pardon me for interrupting you, but doesn't it strike you that this independent American Church, this national church of your dreams, by its very nature will cease to be the *Catholic* church?"

I emphasized the word *Catholic*.

My conversationalist did not grasp it. He continued to develop his thesis with enthusiasm. Unity, according to him, was not an indispensable element. It sufficed that the clergy, the churches, the Mass, and the sacraments would continue to exist. All this was Catholic. Thus America, free and independent, could fly on its own wings, etc., etc.

Since he was speaking in good faith, I attempted to illuminate his somewhat cloudy head. The explanation was long. It was necessary to begin *ab ovo* [from the egg]. He listened to me courteously. In a preachy way, I added that my own personal conviction was that not a single American bishop, either presently or in the future, would enter on the path that he desired. . . .

"Could it be, by chance, that you too are French?" he asked me.

Alas! For all my fine eloquence, and, I must say to my embarrassment, for all my fine logic, the explanation had been a complete fiasco.

I consoled myself for this unpleasantness by reasoning that this profound thinker and brave reformer, who claimed to have received careful training in a religious school, was almost a unique case in this vast country where, it may be, with the lack of deep religious instruction, common sense dominates and rescues orthodoxy.

To arrive at Las Cruces, the departure point for my pastoral tour, I had to cross all of 566 kilometers. In El Paso, where I would arrive at night, I was to change from the Southern Pacific line to the Santa Fe, provided that there were no delays en route.[10]

To miss one's connection in these parts is extremely inconvenient, since the trains come through only once every twenty-four hours. And this was precisely what befell me.

The train, for some reason or another, had been delayed more than usual crossing the deserts of southern Arizona. Long before entering the station at Deming, the first stop in the Territory of New Mexico and 135 kilometers from El Paso, where I was to change trains, I had acquired the certainty, confirmed by the conductor, that we would arrive too late in El Paso to meet the express which climbs the Rio Grande. This would be a shame. Twenty-four hours late.

The following day, a Sunday, they would await me in Las Cruces, where all was ready for the confirmation and where a crowd of Mexicans was to come from five or six leagues in all directions. I began to reflect on ways of circumventing the difficulty, gazing in a melancholy fashion through the transoms as the dry plain fled behind us.

Those who love laughing landscapes would do well to eliminate carefully from their itinerary, to the extent that they have the choice, the crossing of Arizona by the southern line. The appearance of the region is one of savage barrenness. This is the great American desert which no doubt gave its name to this territory: Arizona [the arid zone].[11]

No matter where you may turn your gaze, there are only, as far as the eye can see, empty plains, sandy, alkaline; the reverberation of the sun produces a vast flow of white light that the eye can endure only by blinking strongly. Here and there one sees a few meager tufts of pale sage and cactus of infinite variety. This is the brushland, the steppe, the *llano* of the Mexicans, in a word, the desert. The horizon, just the same, is restful to the gaze. It is invariably closed off by high rocky mountains, naked, of desolate, fierce appearance, but interesting still because of the bizarre silhouettes that they owe to their volcanic origins. In these parts, uninhabited and uninhabitable, these "mesas" mixed with mountains have no names. Only those mountains neighboring some village retain the names with which the ancient Spanish explorers baptized them at the time of the conquest. So these are gracious names, Christian, attesting to the deeply religious state of mind of these great travelers: the mountains of Santa Rita, of Santa Catalina, of Sacramento, of San Simon, San Pedro, Santa Cruz. Most of these peaks are inaccessible. Almost all these mountain chains are virgin still, untrodden by man. No roads, as goes without saying; there are not even any in the plains.

This is the uncontested domain of wild beasts, the home of eagles and vultures, the impenetrable refuge of antelope, deer, and other great game.

Several weeks ago, a Mexican brought to Tucson the hide of a superb jaguar which he had succeeded, with his pack of dogs, in cornering in a cave of the mountain. While the fine dogs, foaming with ardor at the entrance of the cavern, held in check the surprised and stunned beast, the Mexican piled dry branches near the opening and set a fire. This improvised fumigation forced the cat to leave his den. He threw himself through the flames, tore to pieces two or three dogs, and made a dizzy leap toward freedom. The Mexican, a good shot, brought him down in the next instant with a ball from his Winchester. The coat of the animal was magnificent. . . .

They are still asking in Tucson where this carnivore came from and how he came to be there. For while bears are abundant, as well as pumas and wildcats, it is rare indeed to encounter a jaguar.

In the breathless race of our tireless locomotive, pulling behind the enormous weight of eight to ten wagons twenty-five meters long and as heavy as houses, kilometer followed kilometer across the tedious uniformity of the endless plain. The air was suffocating. The dust of the train, mixed with the smoke and fine cinders escaping from the locomotive, stuck to our sweaty faces. Mouths gaping open and arms stretched wide to revive the lungs, the happiest among the travelers snored comfortably, giving no mind to their neighbors. Others, sinking in their seats, limited themselves simply to existing without reading, without speaking, without thinking.

Evidently the monotony of this long afternoon was felt by everyone, overwhelming us all. At rare intervals an incident would shake the general torpor. Sometimes it was a herd of wild horses, crazed by the ship of iron and fleeing breathlessly, manes blowing in the wind, through the brush. At other times, one of those strange happenings unique to this land would attract attention.

At the far end of the plain, giant whirlwinds of dust, straight as columns, would move slowly across the surface of the ground, turning on their axis, pushed through the calm by a mysterious force. On approaching them, one heard a sound like the hissing of a serpent or perhaps similar to miniature waterspouts which sweep the ground in their passage, working the earth in a straight line and displacing the layers of sand.

Everyone has heard about mirages. This aerial phenomenon, rarely observed in Europe, happens every day at many locations in Arizona. Precisely along the route that we were following, there is a point between Lordsburg and Deming where this spectacle is invariably visible.[12] I do not remember having passed by there a single time without seeing it. Beyond the plain, very distant, toward the foot of the mountains, a lake—sometimes a succession of lakes—with clear, tranquil waters bordered by admirable stands of trees, appears to the ravished gaze. The people of the region are not misled by this apparition. But strangers are often fooled. Tormented by thirst and hunger, they lust after the voluptuous thickets with cool shadows, the enticing vision of the Elysian Fields. One person even swore to me that he had seen livestock, roaming freely on the plains in search of a little water, which had allowed themselves to be deceived by these false appearances and had come to die of thirst and exhaustion at the site of the fading gardens.

However accurate this last point may be, it is beyond any doubt that in relatively recent times, among travelers going from Kansas City or Saint Louis to the Pacific Coast, making the trip by cart or on horseback in a company of long caravans forming a convoy to ward off the attacks of the "Redskins," many a miserable soul, delirious from the torture of thirst and of an unrelenting sun and insistent upon pursuing those phantoms retreating before him, has whitened the desert with his bones. . . .[13]

So it goes in this lowly world! Aren't we all, more or less, the victims of deceptive mirages? Misery to him who, allowing himself to be seduced and following foolishly, turns from the true path and goes on to lose himself in these dry and desolate regions without water or pathway, which the scriptures describe as *terra deserta, et invia, et inaquosa!* The most horrible death awaits those strayed from life: death from thirst. The more they rush on in a frenzied race, the more that specious image of false and fleeting happiness which they pursue draws away from them, until finally, discouraged but with their eyes not opened, panting but with their thirst unquenched, they succumb miserably in some solitary place where their friends of a single day have abandoned them.

These reflections have often haunted my soul while traveling through this land of mirages.[14]

One evening just before sunset, as we were approaching Deming, another kind of thought claimed my attention. An immense cloud, thick and black, had suddenly appeared on the eastern horizon. We were traveling straight toward it at full speed. Soon we were in the middle of it. Night fell suddenly. The train's crew hurried to light the lamps, and to lower the windowpanes of the wagons. At the same instant a rain of sleet and sand, an avalanche of dust and grass, battered the windowpanes and the roof with a true fury and with a crackling of hail. We were going, with no more hindrance than ordinary, through one of those sandstorms which reign in the desert during the summer. The day had been one of intense heat, with the oppressive and heavy calm that is the precursor of storms. These hurricanes of sand are sometimes of an extreme violence, carrying off everything in their path, razing hills, changing in an instant, as if by magic, the configuration of the land. During such an incident, livestock surprised by the dizzing rapidity of the storm and unable to escape it by fleeing lie down flat on their bellies, their heads touching the ground. The ponies of the plain do the same. The duration of the tempest is the inverse of its velocity. Generally it passes as it came, suddenly, and one does not know what man or beast may have perished by suffocation.[15]

II

Story of camels.

All these phenomena and many more still, no less strange, evoke, by a natural association of ideas, the memory of descriptions of the Sahara and of the deserts of Arabia which lulled our imaginations in childhood. In fact, the resemblances between the deserts that I traverse and the great African deserts are so numerous and so exact that all travelers are struck by them. Often, one might believe that he was in the Mideast. This is notably the case in the old *haciendas* and the Spanish *pueblos* which have survived the invasion of the Territory by the Anglo-Saxon element.

The first American settlers, who penetrated Arizona some fifty years ago, experienced this resemblance to Arabian deserts to such a point that they got it in their heads to introduce and utilize, in the Arabian tradition, the camel and the dromedary. The story of this attempt, which turned out badly, is both epic and humorous.

The first to conceive the idea was none other than the illustrious Jefferson Davis, later named President of the Southern Confederacy. This was in 1851; the session of Congress was coming to an end, and those gentlemen in the Senate, as happens elsewhere, were hurrying carelessly through the budget. Under cover of the unanimous haste to approve all proposed expenditures, at the last moment Mr. Davis, then senator from the State of Mississippi, introduced a bill authorizing the purchase and importation of thirty camels, ten dromedaries, ten or twelve Arabian camel handlers, and all the necessary equipment.

In his persuasive arguments, the senator emphasized the great services that these animals rendered as pack animals in Asia and Africa; in India, the English used them to transport war supplies and even small cannons. Napoleon used them in Egypt in his disputes with a race similar to the Apaches and Comanches. These four-legged beasts would thus be of the greatest utility in the wars with the Redskins of the Far West. Laying in a supply of water sufficient for a distance of 100 miles, and running without respite at a speed of 12 to 15 miles an hour, they could, he said, easily catch up to the bands of Indians escaping the cavalry. They would be used to carry small caliber pieces. In a word, they would be used with the same success as had been experienced in the Mideast. There, they were accustomed to living on underbrush and were content to drink a brackish water similar to that found in the American West.

The introduction of innovations in the army, as commendable as they may be, is a hard job in any country. Senator Davis's idea was treated by several of his colleagues as a baroque eccentricity. To invest $30,000 to this end would be, they said, an extravagance that the taxpayers would never forgive the Senate. The proposition was defeated by a large majority.

Nevertheless, the press took up the project again surreptitiously. The California newspapers began to raise the issue, and soon public opinion was excited. The partisans of the dromedaries argued that one could organize an extremely rapid postal service: mail from the East, they said, would arrive in California within fifteen days. It would be just as easy to create express convoys of camels to transport travelers in very little time from the banks of the Missouri to the coast of the Pacific. Nothing could be more natural: the animals would fill their internal reservoirs with water from the Missouri, strike out straight ahead toward the

West, and in exchange for a few meals grabbed hastily in the underbrush, could wait with no problem to renew their water supply upon reaching the banks of the Colorado River. From there, they would make a new dash toward the West, and in less than two weeks, the traveler from the banks of the Missouri would be deposited fresh and spruce at his destination, one of several cities along the coast of the Pacific. No need, in order to arrive in California, to risk one's life through exposure to the fevers of Panama and the thievery of the natives of the Isthmus. No need to expose oneself to death from thirst during the desert crossing or to die of cold while traversing the icy summits of the Rocky Mountains. The two-step caravan which the convoy of camels would form would remedy all that, thus resolving the problem of rapid transport across the Far West while the nation was awaiting the construction of the transcontinental railroad.

The insistence of the press, and its arguments along commercial lines, produced more effect on the Senate than the patriotic abjurations of strategic order presented by Mr. Davis. In December 1854, the Captain Major C. Wayne received orders to go to Egypt and Arabia to make the purchase of seventy-five camels at government expense. In Cairo the Captain bought forty-five, loaded them on board the transport *Supply,* and set a course for Smyrna. There he chose thirty more camels of a different species that had served in the deserts of Arabia, paying from $75 to $300 a head. The *Supply* reached Indianola, Texas, with its cargo of camels on February 10, 1857. Three camels had perished at sea, leaving a total of seventy-two magnificent beasts.

Half were brought to Albuquerque, New Mexico, where a trial expedition was immediately organized under the command of Lieutenant Beale, with a destination of Fort Tejon, California. The route followed the 35th parallel, traversing the Mohave Desert to the Northwest of Arizona. The caravan comprised forty-four travelers escorted by a detachment of twenty soldiers, with the camels carrying the baggage and the supply of potable water.

The troop arrived safely at Tejon, and several trips were carried out afterwards between Fort Tejon and Albuquerque.

The other half of the troop had been directed to the South of Arizona and served as the transportation of supplies and ammunition intended for the military forts established in these regions to defend them against the Apaches. Each animal carried a load of 1,000 to 2,000 English pounds, and with this load covered from forty-five to fifty kilometers a day, finding what was needed for subsistence in the most arid plains and going from six to ten days without drinking. The largest and strongest could, with a load of 2,000 pounds, maintain a speed of twenty-five kilometers an hour.

Everything went well at the beginning, and one might have believed that the problem of rapid and low-cost communication across the great plains had finally found a happy solution.

But a mistake had been made, a serious mistake, although still reparable. Along with the camels from the Mideast, no one had remembered to import the Arabian camel handlers. This mistake became the cause of tribulations without number and caused an enterprise, otherwise attractive and worthy of a better fate, to fail lamentably.

Homesick and dumbfounded at their arrival in America after long months of difficult sailing, the poor beasts had appeared, at first encounter, to be gentle, docile, and entirely passive. Nevertheless, as time went by, between the camel and the Yankee muledriver there developed a mutual antipathy which, instead of smoothing out with daily commerce, only became aggravated.

To succeed in the art of managing camels, one must be born a camel handler. This unique talent, which dates from a thousand years and more, since it goes back to the time of Abraham and Isaac, must be passed on from father to son.

The first source of misunderstanding between the two was language. The vehement invectives and the barbaric oaths of the ex-muledrivers irritated the nerves and shocked the *delicatesse* of the Arabian camels, who no doubt had never in their lives heard echoing in their ears anything other than *"Allah el' Allah"* spoken in the suavest Arabian accent. In turn, the passive indolence of the camels irritated the conductors.

They understood and appreciated the vigorous bucks of their former beasts of burden, the Army mules, when those animals, dissatisfied, wanted to protest. But the melancholy despondence and the soft and dull eyes of these Oriental beasts exasperated them. They were not long in realizing, moreover, that, by nasty little tricks, a single camel could give its master more thread to wind than a whole batallion of mules.

When, toward evening, the hour for pitching camp arrived, the camels were relieved of their packsaddles and left to themselves to gnaw on prickly cactus for their dinner. Then, whether it was to escape from the tumult of the other camels and the oaths of the soldiers, or whether it was to see the countryside, they never failed to allow themselves an additional stroll of twenty-five to thirty kilometers before the meal. The drivers spent half their time chasing them.

Another problem. The camels could cart enormous stacks of baggage, but when two "ships of the desert," heavily loaded, collided in a narrow passage, their loads scattered across the plain and the camel handlers never finished gathering them up again.

As the final misery, the aversion the men had for these biblical animals was shared fully by the cavalry of the forts. Every time that one of these long-legged and humped beasts passed by an infantry squad, or else, in the calm of the evening, let loose one of those fantastic shrieks of which camels alone possess the secret, the entire cavalry took flight in a dreadful panic.

For all these reasons, Uncle Sam's military ended up detesting the poor camels and mistreated them cheerfully. In vain the officers demanded that the men make new attempts at handling them. The men mutinied, declaring that not a single military law existed requiring them to be camel drivers. Expert teamsters were engaged; they deserted at the end of one day. Thus, lacking arms to load and pilot these "caravels of the desert," the crossings were made less and less frequently and soon ceased completely.

So ends the story of this Homeric attempt at camel domestication in the Far West. As for the unfortunate specimens of an exotic race, they ended up in a still sadder fashion. Rather than the camels chasing Apaches as Senator Davis had dreamed, it was the "Redskins" who set themselves to chasing the camels. A goodly number terminated their existence in a manner hardly heroic, on the grill or in the stew pot of some "wigwam Indian." Others perished by the bullets of soldiers sent to pursue them when they strayed into the neighborhood.

The last survivors, after numerous adventures, were totally abandoned one fine day and left in the desert. In 1882 some were found living in a wild condition in Arizona; some enterprising industrialists followed them, caught them with lassoes, and sold them to a menagerie. Still, a small number survived all these trials and continue to wander across the desert regions of Arizona and Sonora. Several years ago, the International Commission charged with surveying the border between the Union and Mexico noted the finding of wild camels in its official report. These must be the descendants of the imported group, for they seem to be in the prime of life. Only—no doubt the effect of adaptation to the environment—they were completely white.[16]

III

Continuation of trip by train. Stop at Rincón.
Arrival in Las Cruces.

Five-thirty in the evening—Deming! A twenty-minute stop and three hours behind schedule. I will certainly miss, at El Paso, the train for Las Cruces.

Resigning myself poorly to the prospect of languishing for twenty-four hours while waiting for the next train and thus missing my meeting in Las Cruces on Sunday, I went to the information booth and, to my great satisfaction, learned that a local train was going to leave Deming at 9:00 in the evening, going Northeast. This train would pass at about midnight through Rincón, a small station located fifty-three kilometers north of Las Cruces. I quickly decided to take advantage of this. Doubtless this was taking the schoolboy's route, going North in order to come back down South later. But at Rincón, if the train from Santa Fe was not delayed, it would pick me up in passage at 7:00 in the morning and drop me off at Las Cruces around 9:00, in time for Mass and confirmation.

With three hours before me, I renewed my acquaintance with the small town of Deming, lost in the middle of the desert.[17] I knew it from long ago. The plateau on which the village is scattered is located not far from the opening of the narrow valley of Mimbres. From this valley descends a river of pure water which, upon reaching the plain, is lost in the sands.[18]

At this site, water is abundant several feet below ground. Each house is supplied with a pump, worked by an iron windmill, coming from factories in Chicago.

This forest of windmills rising on all sides above the houses would give, at first glance, the illusion of a Dutch hamlet if it were not for the absence of the canals and verdant meadows which constitute the beauty and richness of the Netherlands. Here the wooden houses are built in sand; streets are traced in sand. Not a blade of grass is to be seen. The only green growth is the pale green underbrush of the plain.

When it has calmed elsewhere, the wind still blows two days later in Deming because of the village's exposed position in the middle of a plateau. Sandstorms are frequent here. But since, thanks to the altitude, the temperature is relatively mild, the inhabitants of this town, lost in the desert and inhabited primarily by cowboys and cattlemen, live here without complaining. We still do not have a chapel in this locale. A priest comes every month from seventy-seven kilometers away to say Mass in a home and administer the sacraments.

Night has fallen. After a hearty supper at the excellent railroad hotel, I board the train, which starts off shortly after 9:00 p.m. Almost no passengers are aboard.

When I ask the conductor at which inn I will be able to rest upon my arrival in Rincón in the middle of the night, he informs me that there are no inns. He promises to entrust me to a worthy gentleman of his acquaintance who will find me shelter. The night, moonless, is black as ink. To pass the time, I deliver myself over to personal meditation. . . .

Shortly before midnight the train stops at a seemingly deserted place. Not a movement, not a light. This is Rincón.[19] The conductor, an obliging man, searches in the dark for the silhouette of his friend. Finding him, the conductor recommends me to his friend's good caretaking, and starts the train in motion again in the direction of the North.

My host, a tall, thin, old man, face decorated by a disheveled beard, makes a sign to follow him. He lights a lantern and off we go, one behind the other, across mounds of sand. I vaguely distinguish branches of tall trees. We arrive at a small house made of wooden boards. My companion ushers me into a small chamber three-fourths occupied by a large bed and wishes me good night. He will wake me in the morning in time for the train which will take me to Las Cruces. Since it is hot and it still is not midnight, I ask him if I may have some refreshment. With alacrity, he brings me a glass of warm, yellow water, which, for want of anything better, I swallow gratefully.

Toward 5:00 in the morning I am awakened by loud blows on my door. Someone wants to speak with me. I cover myself hastily and, opening the door, find myself face to face with an American.

"Good day, Father. At what time are you saying the Mass?"

"But, how was I to know that you would like to have Mass this morning in Rincón? At 7:00 I take the train for Las Cruces. . . ."

"Oh, yes! It seems that they're expecting the bishop there today. I would very much like to go. He's a new bishop; I have never seen him."

"Oh, but you have, my good man; you have spoken to him; you know him perfectly."

The good man went off dumbfounded, not comprehending what I was trying to say.

Toward 7:00 I take the train which, happily, is not delayed this morning, and at full steam we descend into the valley of the Rio Grande, which I had reached during the night. Tall trees border the riverbed, which is almost dry everywhere. Wild ducks take flight noisily at our passage. There are enough to delight a legion of hunters. But in these solitary parts, no one disturbs them.

The morning is fresh and gay; the sun bursting but gentle; the air light and completely pure. Green growth spreads all along the bed of the Rio Grande, which flows at our side along the speedy course of the train. All this, mixed with the lively pleasure I feel at arriving on time for the meeting, makes me forget quickly the terrible previous day in the great reaches of sand, and the sandstorm, and the ardent thirst, and the sleep that was a little too light and too short in the shaky double bed of my host in Rincón.

I had taken care the evening before to advise the parish priest of Las Cruces, "don Pedro," by telegram of my arrival. Don Pedro is a Lyonnais of whom we will later make ample acquaintance. We speed through the little stations of Tonuco and Doña Ana, and at 9:00 we arrive at Las Cruces, the point of departure for my tour of confirmation.[20]

IV

Solemn reception. Indian dances. A lively confirmation.

Don Pedro, although somewhat taken aback by this arrival at an unexpected hour, had arranged things well.

Early in the morning the bell of his little church had called together the faithful; they had spread the news, and upon my descent from the train, I find myself facing a large part of the population coming to meet me. Don Pedro shakes my hand strongly by way of greeting, then presents me to the crowd, which rushes forward to kiss my ring. But time passes; the bell, in the distance, announces loud and clear the hour of the High Mass.

The church is located a kilometer from the train station. I am seated in a cart with benches, and the parade begins: the women and children on foot, through the dust, and the men on horseback. Just in front of my carriage, which advances majestically at a walk, an entire tribe of Indians and squaws executes, as in the time of David, a sacred dance. There they are heads bare, a row of men, a row of women, alternately, their faces decorated with red ochre, their bodies covered with furs of wild animals or cottons in bright colors, their feet covered with mocassins. A drum beats the rhythm. With their hollow voices, the "Redskins" roll out musical phrases to the Indian taste, which a composer of the Conservatory would have trouble recognizing. Two or three notes constitute the range of this bizarre chant of a primitive, prehistoric simplicity. The total effect produced is of a deafening buzz, hammered out and taken up, at equal intervals, by crescendos completely unexpected. The steps follow the beat; and half dancing, half jumping, breaking ranks in cadence so as to change place by running back and forth, the corps de ballet advances slowly, raising a cloud of dust at its passage. The good bourgeoisie of the place come to their doors, curious and sympathetic. The innumerable dogs of the village are all there, barking, making a frightening ruckus. . . .[21]

We arrive at the plaza of the church.[22] The Indian chorus installs itself at the entrance of the temple and for another quarter of an hour drums, hums, jumps, and dances, celebrating the great day in its own manner. The leader, a large, sturdy fellow, who carries hanging from his arms the hats of all the participants, beats the rhythm tirelessly. These good Indians, grave, impassive, with long, angular, beardless faces in which not a muscle moves, their gazes fixed before them upon the great altar all blazing with lights at the end of the nave, continue their choreographic cycles. All at once, suddenly and without finale, song and dance stop in a final purr. Breathless, bathed with sweat, the dancers retire in good order. Good children of nature, the Lord will have contemplated favorably the sincerity of your hearts and the form, strange but deliciously naive, of its expression. . . .

From where do these Indians come? From three or four miles down the river, where they possess several plots of land which furnish them subsistence. They are all Catholic. Sadly, their ranks are seeing the light from one day to the next, and soon their *cachinas*, or religious dances, will be no more than a distant memory. The conditions of modern life in America are poorly adapted to the ways of these sons of the desert. They suffer, they languish, and too often, alas! at the contact of the whites, they drift into a way of life which is not at all made for them and which demoralizes them.[23]

The confirmation ceremony was to take place following High Mass. The church, too narrow for the occasion, overflowed with people. Four-fifths were Mexicans or mestizos. This was apparent from the tanned complexions, the shining black eyes, the abundant ebony hair, and the brightly colored outfits. A small number were Americans from all parts of the Union. The American has learned the nomadic practices of the Indian. It costs him nothing to abandon his place of birth in order to search for more in the new regions of the Far West or elsewhere. In fact, very few among them remain in their paternal homes, and once departed thence, they settle nowhere. The trunk is always ready for a new move. For a song, they go to live at the other end of the country, and then leave to come back or to try somewhere else.

Since the audience was mixed, it was a matter of my addressing them in two languages, English and Spanish. I began with Spanish. The short speech was given without incident before an attentive audience, but I had scarcely begun my discourse in English, for those who did not understand Spanish, when I perceived among the Mexican ranks some kind of growing agitation. Men and women were rising, leaving their benches, going from here to there, passing by each other. Uncooperative babies soon began to scream their heads off and fill the church with a deafening commotion. In these former Spanish colonies, it is the custom to confirm the children at a young age. When all is said and done, confirmation of adults is rare and generally is limited to Americans. The Mexicans treat confirmation like baptism and have it administered to young babies. Moreover, each child is furnished with a godfather or godmother according to its sex. To be invited to serve as godfather is considered a great honor and a sign of deep friendship. It establishes, from that moment, between the godparents and parents of the child tight, strong bonds which cause the godfather to be considered as a member of the family, and he is treated as such until death. The institution of *compadres* and *comadres* is universal among the Mexicans; it fills their lives with an important role, and they value it like the pupils of their eyes.

You can ask any service whatsoever of your *compadre;* it will not be denied. Your house is his; your belongings are at his disposition. These multiple attachments, mostly between families, maintain the unity of the Mexican population and permit them to resist, to a certain extent, the invasions of the Anglo-Saxon race. The Mexicans who live in the United States do not bother to learn the language of the country, which is English, and continue to observe their own traditions and customs as they did before the annexation of their lands by the American Union.

There were that morning, in the little church of Las Cruces, several hundred youngsters wailing at the top of their lungs. I was forced to complete my speech in English by raising my voice to its highest pitch. Still I was defeated; after several fruitless attempts, I observed that I was no longer heard, and I had to resign myself to completing my sermon, a tidbit, moreover, that I had especially polished, by means of an eloquent mime and desolate gestures.

The confirmation ceremony lasted a good hour. The babies revolted. The children of three and four were the worst. They stamped their feet with fright, while the godparents, somewhat awkwardly, and the mothers hidden behind could not succeed in calming them. For the frontal blessing, Don Pedro often had to hold them by the hair until I could apply the holy oils. Several pushed me away with their hands when I approached, kicking at my surplice and showing signs of great fright. Others wanted to bite me. The mingled cries of all these little rascals could have made one honestly believe that it was a Massacre of the Innocents. I never have understood what can cause such terror among these youngsters at the moment of confirmation. Try as you may to give yourself a smiling, sweet expression, it is in vain. The first cries issuing from some part of the crowd cause the dust to fly, and the clamor redoubles on all sides. It is, no doubt, a case of panic or fear by contagion. But the ceremony, under these conditions, is always quite tiring to the nervous system; one must arm oneself, before beginning, with a strong resolution to proceed, no matter what happens, with an imperturbable calm, an absolute impassiveness.

When everything is finished, the mammas gather up the babies, calm their crying, and dry the little cheeks flowing with sweat and tears. The godfather and all the family return home joyful and content, determined to celebrate "twice in twenty-four hours" the beauty and sweetness of *compadrazgo*.[24]

V

The dean of Arizona missionaries. Visit to the convent of the Sisters of Las Cruces. The visit of the Rio Grande. Protestantism. Story of Jacinto.

I allow myself after lunch, in one of the clean rooms of Don Pedro, two hours of well-deserved rest, Don Pedro offering me hospitality in a brick house that he had constructed just by the church. The front, on the west side, boasts a porch or veranda where climbing plants offer cool shade. The church, also the work of Don Pedro, is of brick, topped by a beautiful bell and dedicated to Saint Geneviève.[25] In the courtyard of the rectory I notice several grapevine stocks and a successful planting of fig trees. A windmill collects in an iron reservoir the water necessary for the household, the garden, and the horses which I see resting in a corner of the corral.

Don Pedro is the dean of the Arizona missionaries.[26] Coming into these missions as a very young priest at the time of Monseigneur Lamy, thirty-seven years ago, he has grown old under the harness. But his heart remains young, brave, and joyous. He knew dangers, miseries, and deprivations of the first order at the time when Arizona had not yet been set up as an apostolic bishopric. At that time the country was infested with rebellious Indians. One only traveled armed to the teeth, and preferably at night, since the "Redskins" were supposed never to attack during darkness. The trip from Mississippi to Arizona took months, traveling across the great plains and mountains by wagon train or on horseback. Don Pedro could have filled a thick book with the stories of his various adventures. Most of his first companions are now dead. He himself has survived all trials, and despite the weight of his years, he is still zealous, ardent, very pious, very devout, still happy and gay. He is the idol of his flock, and the good he has accomplished in the mission is incalculable. What good and fine missionaries France has given these distant missions for the past half century! The Latin blood and Gallic character adapt perfectly to apostleship in Mexican lands. Were it not for the admirable work of these valiant apostles, the mestizos, left to themselves without guidance, would long ago have lost the faith and reverted to a near-savage state.[27]

At 4:00 in the afternoon, a new confirmation ceremony for those who, coming from afar, had not arrived in time for the morning confirmation. New confusion, new uproar, but this time less well nourished than in the morning, since the crowd is less numerous.

The ceremony completed, a buggy takes me to the other end of town to the private boarding school kept by the Sisters of Loretto.[28] The construction, already old, is of good appearance. The academy is flourishing. It numbers forty residents, among whom are several who have come from Mexico. All this little world is assembled in a room to wish me welcome. The Protestant students—there are always a certain number—show as much respect and pleasure as their Catholic companions.

One of them, newly converted, was baptized and made her first communion a few days ago. I give her confirmation.

Of all the arts of pleasure, music is by far the most enjoyed in these regions. No child comes through the academy without leaving more or less a musician. While they prepare a small, impromptu concert, I complete my tour of the establishment, clear to the top floor and even up to the attic, for at this height we enjoy a magnificent view. A gallery extends the entire length of the side facing South.

The valley of the Rio Grande unfurls as far as the eye can see in green cultivation where alfalfa dominates, a kind of lucerne (*Medicago sativa*). This hardy grass is almost the sole fodder harvested in Arizona. It grows abundantly in the alluvial lands everywhere that irrigation is possible, for here we must not count on rains: they are almost nonexistent. But in soil maintained in a relatively humid condition, the sun and the continuous heat take care of the rest; harvests are abundant and multiple; such a meadow gives up to seven cuttings. A ton of alfalfa sells, according to the season, for $12 to $18.

Shady gardens alternate with the alfalfa plantations, orchards where the fig tree and the pomegranate spread out exuberantly. Here and there, green masses of cottonwood trees, with their immense branches, enchant the gaze. The cottonwood (*Populus monilifera*), of the willow family, called "tree of cotton," takes its name from the cottony envelope which encloses the seed. It is, without argument, the most beautiful tree among the Arizona flora. Everywhere that its roots encounter a moist undersoil, the cottonwood tree attains superb dimensions. Its foliage is very dense and of a beautiful green; the vast shade that it projects is deliciously cool. Lacking the palm of the Mideast, the great, burning plains of Arizona offer here and there to the weary traveler the welcome shelter of a solitary cottonwood. Thus it is that Dame Nature, sometimes grumpy and miserly, at other times provides a few sweetnesses in the most underprivileged regions for the inhabitants of the earth, as if seized by pity for them.

This part of the Rio Grande Valley, of which I glimpse a small section from the top of my observatory and which I will follow to El Paso, is truly a delicious oasis. The river which serves it was named by the Spanish *Rio Grande del Norte* [the Great River of the North], an appropriate name, for with the exception of the Mississippi, the Rio Grande is the longest course of water in America.

From its source in the Colorado mountains to its mouth in the Gulf of Mexico, the Rio Grande forms an artery 3,000 kilometers long. At its upper part, its current is enclosed in a narrow basin, closed at places by *cañones*, or deep gorges.

As it gains the South, the river extends its bed and flows in the middle of a wide valley. Sadly, on such a long journey, its volume of water, which it owes principally to the melting of snows, is gradually diminished, whether by diversion for irrigation of river land, or by infiltration into the sand, or, finally, by the considerable evaporation that it undergoes in a heated atmosphere almost entirely deprived of humidity. Thus the populations settled along the banks of the Rio Grande see their prosperity decrease from day to day. Most of the time the river bed is dry, and serves as a road for vehicles.

"Times are bad along the Rio Grande," is heard on all sides.[29]

What is no less regrettable than the chronic drought of the river is the bad habit that it has, during great overflows, of suddenly transporting its bed elsewhere. You camp, for example, one evening on the banks of the river, and the next morning you see it flowing by several hundred meters from your campsite.

Despite all these inconveniences, the Valley of the Rio Grande, inhabited since long ago, continues to nourish a large part of the population of New Mexico. The Mexican families who have established their homes here generally remain faithful to the land. This is not exactly the Valley of the Nile, but for the poor mestizos, accustomed to a hard life, it is something approaching it.

While I feast my eyes on this restful landscape from the top of the house, the young residents, having tuned their instruments, cast the first notes of the concert to the evening breeze. One of them plays the piano; the others, arranged in a semicircle, strum the strings of gaily beribboned guitars and mandolines. They played several pieces with a perfect spirit. This melodious music, sweet and caressing, harmonizes beautifully with the calm reigning all around during this peaceful end to a beautiful day. I compliment the young artists warmly, by way of encouragement, and take up again the route to the rectory, where supper awaits me.

After the meal, the devotional exercise of the Month of Mary takes place, a devotion imported from France by the missionaries and dear to the Mexicans. The church is filled once more. Before the altar of the good Mother, children clothed in white graciously toss flowers at the foot of the sacred image, while another group of young girls sings in chorus the Gloria Patri of each ten-line stanza.[30]

Everywhere that the devotion to Mary is honored, faith is maintained and victoriously resists the attacks of Protestantism. At Las Cruces, defections are rare among the Mexicans. In a few isolated cases, unfortunate ones allow themselves to be led astray, seduced by a sordid bait. But almost invariably, on their deathbeds, they reject the Protestant minister and implore, with loud cries, the aid and the pardons of the Catholic church.

Among the Mexicans, the church is still the uncontested queen of their existence. Its life is their life; its joys are their feast days; its laws, the rule of their conduct. At the end of the celebration of the Month of Mary, a mestizo and a woman come to consult me about a matter of marriage which is bothering them badly and making them very unhappy. Humble and submissive, they await my decision, responding with the greatest candor to the questions I ask them. The case is simple to resolve; I am happy to send them off to their home consoled and moved. Truly, the work of the first Spanish missionaries, companions of Cortés, among this ancient race of the Aztecs is something to be admired. The faith which they planted in the heart of this race, then wild, shy, and sanguine, has issued forth from such deep roots that the revolutions without number which have shaken and bloodied this unhappy and beautiful land during the course of the centuries have not succeeded in making a dent in it.

For a long time the biblical societies of New England have worked to "pluck these good Mexican populations from the shameful yoke of papism." Each year they send bands of missionaries loaded with gold and astounding promises.[31] These missionaries, in general, show nothing for their proselytising efforts; nevertheless, they well resist complaining about their lack of success: the country is beautiful, the climate agreeable, the life sweet. They are fatly salaried, and although their existence may be a perfect sinecure, to the touched eyes of their naive patrons, they appear crowned with the glories of apostleship, whose luster they take great care to maintain by means of marvelous reports. A few poor, famished wretches come, it is true, to place themselves under their shepherds' crooks. But these are, as always, "the weeds of its garden that the Church throws over the hedge." The reform minister obtains from his flock no recompense other than the gratitude of their stomachs.

At the time when, as a simple missionary, I made monthly visits to the town of Nogales on the Mexican border, one of my faithful was a fine mestizo who served me as sexton. He was alone in the world, old, crippled with infirmities; life was painful for him. Religion was his sole sustenance and consolation. So he never missed the call, and the only happy moments of his poor existence were those he spent each month in my company in service at the altar.

One fine day I did not see the faithful Jacinto arrive.

Fearing illness, I went looking for information. Alas! My former sexton had made himself into a Protestant! In exchange for 50 sous, he swept the sermon room, sounded the bells, and awakened the parish. A few supplies of flour, sugar, and coffee would come from time to time to tell him of the gratitude of his devoted pastor and the beauties of his new *Credo*.

Poor Jacinto! Months passed without my seeing him. I always suspected that he kept himself perfectly informed about the date of my visits to the town and abstained from going out then, for fear of meeting me.

One morning, arriving at my church at daybreak, I stumbled against some formless thing huddled on the doorstep. A moan escaped, the mass rose slowly, and I recognized Jacinto. He held himself there without a word, head lowered, with a grieved air, ashamed and embarrassed.

"Well, my fine Jacinto, from where have you come, then? It's been a century since I've seen you! I thought you were dead. . . ."

"Ah! *Padre, Usted dice bien.* [Yes, you are indeed correct.] I was dead, and worse, even."

"The devil! This is serious. What in the world took place?"

I already had the pardon on my lips, but the confession of the guilty one was needed.

"Ah! *Padre, Usted dice muy bien.* Yes, the devil! It is he who is the cause of everything. He rendered me *burro* [dumb as a jackass], and I have done foolish things. Several days ago, I almost died. He was there, the minister, or perhaps the devil getting ready to carry off my old carcass into the earth. . . ."

And saying this, the poor man delivered great blows upon his chest with his fist.

"But I did not want it," he added tearfully. "I was afraid of dying without you. . . . Ah! What a *burro* I am! *María santissima,* have pity on me!"

Another series of blows with the fist to his stomach, which sounded frightfully hollow.

"It's all right, my son!" I replied, "you are repentant. God pardons you. But, truly, what were you doing in that gallery of rogues!"

"Misery, *Padre de mi alma,* misery and famine, faulty counsel. . . ."

The chagrin of the poor old man was painful to see. I took him affectionately by the shoulder and consoled him, as did, in olden days, the father of the prodigal child. Having neither a fatted calf to sacrifice nor a golden ring to slip on his finger, I did my best to celebrate in a worthy manner his return to the cradle.

Jacinto was not long in going to his last sleep in the tomb of his fathers. The compassionate Father whom we have in heaven will have gathered up, in His mercy, his tears of repentance; and the old sexton of Nogales, who in his mortal life knew only the privations of misery and ate his bread soaked in tears, now drinks in long drafts, let us hope, at the fountain of delights in the land of the living.

VI

⚱

"In terra deserta, invia et inaquosa." Father Jean. Confirmation at Mesilla.

The day following this happy Sunday spent in Las Cruces, after a restoring sleep I arise fresh and fit, ready to continue my route along the Rio Grande, destination La Mesilla. Toward 9:30 I pack my bags and climb into the carriage for La Mesilla, accompanied by Don Pedro. Two good horses belonging to the Sisters pull our coach. The distance to travel, moreover, is minimal: five kilometers at the most.

Las Cruces and La Mesilla are the sole parishes of the Tucson diocese which are, to some extent, neighboring. Generally, the residences of the missionaries are separated by hundreds of kilometers. This exception of Las Cruces and La Mesilla traces its origin to times past when the course of the river separated the two locales. The waters then were more abundant and the floods of longer duration, and often the Rio Grande remained uncrossable for weeks, for there was never any bridge.

Since that time, the river, following its old habits, has judged it appropriate to transport its bed some kilometers to the west, leaving the two parishes on the left bank. The former bed has become a *route royale*.[32]

The road that we follow, also a royal road [*camino real*], would be classified as a by-road in Europe. The very wise institution called macadam—from the name of its Scottish inventor—is absolutely unknown in the western United States.[33] In Arizona, notably, where nineteen-twentieths of the land is unoccupied, the field is free. Pedestrians, horsemen, and vehicles go where it seems best. By virtue of the principle of a straight line constituting the shortest path, it happens habitually that once a footpath or wagon route is traced from one point to another, it is then taken up by the travelers who follow, and *voilà*—the road is made; even if later you have to abandon it and launch out into the brush should another trail seem better or more direct to you. It follows that roads worthy of the name do not exist in these parts.

The road to Mesilla is rather a daredevil road. The potholes, treacherously disguised under unbelievable thicknesses of dust, put our axles in danger at each instant. The violent shocks and brusque jolts slow our journey, singularly facilitating, moreover, our digestive functions.

Our valiant little horses advance cheerfully without troubling themselves about the roughness of the road. The best course to follow is to do the same, and laughing all the while about the jostling that cannot be resisted, we find compensation for our troubles in the interesting aspects of the places through which we are traveling.

To our left, very distant, the horizon to the east is shut off by immense masses of rocks with picturesque, carved crests. These are the *Organos* [mountains of the pipe organs], whose reddish silhouettes rise up against a blue background, juxtaposed with spurts of prismatic rocks, vaguely reminiscent of the pipes of a gigantic pipe organ. The Organs form a point of departure in the region that is visible from great distances, thanks to the perfect clearness of the air.[34] On this side of the mountains, the terrain, arid and desolate, declines in a gentle slope to the edge of the valley proper, vibrant with light and life under a blinding sun.

At the end of the village, Don Pedro shows me, behind a thick curtain of osage-orange trees, or arcwood (*Maclura auran-*

tiaca), a piece of land, property of the church, where formerly there was a small vineyard from which he took his wine for mass.

At first, everything went well, and the harvests were good. Then marauders joined the party, and grapes disappeared nightly, although still green and good for nougat candy. Out of patience, the good abbot decided reluctantly to apply an heroic remedy. One fine morning, he pulled up all the vine stocks and put alfalfa in their place. This latter crop, of a culture less fruitful but also less difficult and less tempting, consoles him generously, moreover, for the loss of his beloved vineyard, for it grows abundantly dense and shining.

Here and there emerge the heads of horses and cattle plunged chest-high into alfalfa. The fields of wheat, barley, and corn ripple in the breeze as far as the eye can see on both sides of the road. This alluvial soil, assisted by the productive action of a sun which shines invariably twelve hours each day in a sky that is always serene, is so rich and naturally fertile that, without the assistance of the slightest amount of fertilizer, it gives early and abundant harvests, on the condition, however, that sufficient irrigation joins with the sun to impregnate it.[35]

We traverse the former bed of the Rio Grande and enter into the territory of Mesilla. Large spaces, planted in orchards, border the road at different points, or else appear far off forming great squares of green. A few solitary houses, lost in the fields, appear one by one, then closer together, and soon we see, several paces from us, a clustering of low houses half hidden in the trees, a little steeple emerging from the middle of the flat roofs forming the housetops. At the pace of the horses splashing knee-high in the dust, we make our entry, modest and dignified, into the town of Mesilla.[36]

Father Jean, the missionary here, not expecting us before the afternoon, is at his house some distance from the church. We go to surprise him. A welcome in the French manner, expansive and cordial, makes us forget in a wink of the eye our multiple contusions, the inevitable results of the immoderate jostlings of our cart. Once a little glass of *chimaga*, a cordial invented by the Indians and made with a balsam grass of the desert, has clarified our thoughts, we put ourselves to the task of arranging the day's disposition.[37]

The confirmation will take place at 4:00 in the afternoon, when the greatest blast of heat should have passed. For the late arrivals there will be another confirmation the following day, after the Mass.

Between the two, free time and rest; handling business which might present itself; visiting the school and the community of the Sisters of Mercy who direct it; and finally, becoming acquainted with the environment and the promenades around the village.

While awaiting the dinner hour, I make the rounds of the rectory. It is a large house, made of earth, without a second story, and consisting of a half dozen vast rooms, well aired and whitened with lime. It was built some thirty years ago by Father Morin, who intended to make it the novitiate of the diocese's Sisters of Mercy. A small garden fronts it, opening onto the street. Behind and on one side is a piece of land sowed or planted as an orchard. A well, not very deep, furnishes the household's water, and is never dry. A large courtyard, or corral, serves as a home for poultry and for a pair of horses that I see grinding peacefully on corn husks.

This residence is reputed to be one of the best in the diocese.[38] Its occupant, a native son of Auvergne, vigorous and of an iron constitution, for many years has presided over the spiritual destinies of the Mexican villages in this part of the Rio Grande. Not very familiar with English, he speaks Castillian as if it were his mother tongue. In contrast to Don Pedro, who is a poet on his own time, Father Jean has a mathematical mind. He excels in the arts of precision: in turn clockmaker, sculptor, woodcarver, mechanic, it is he who constructed the altars of his chapels, turned the candlesticks that one admires, and sculpted the crucifix that decorates his room. In his leisure hours he is a bookbinder: all the books in his small library have been bound by his own hands. What is more, as an able blacksmith, he himself makes his tools, and I have a vague memory that in the past he cast the bells for his missions.

After dinner he shows us the canons of the altar, superbly illuminated on parchment in the style of the Middle Ages.

"This is a work of my youth!" he tells us modestly.

Nevertheless, as it is a very beautiful work and I admire it, he graciously makes me a gift of it. This precious ornament will perpetuate, in the cathedral of Tucson, the memory of Father Jean, a great artist and valiant missionary.[39]

Four o'clock. The bells of the little church of La Mesilla announce loud and clear the confirmation ceremony. Father Jean is already at the post, in the sacristy, registering the names of those to be confirmed and of their respective godparents. A few have come from everywhere, as attested to by the carts and saddled mounts which are lined all along the length of the streets. I set off on the path of fine sand which leads from the rectory to the church, extricating myself with great difficulty and risking leaving my shoe in some pothole at each instant. Finally, here is the church, at the end of a large plaza planted with trees.

The crowd is stationed at the entrance awaiting the bishop, who arrives alone without drums or trumpets, shaking the dust from his habit and wiping his face. Fortunately, I do not have a "master of ceremonies" at my heels! The walk in the dust under the full sun has put me in a state which does some little harm to my decorum. What would you ask? One does what one can. I verify, moreover, by a rapid look at the crowd, that my appearance, by comparison, is among the most acceptable, and that this sentiment is shared by all present.

The ranks open, and a line forms at my passage. As I arrive at the threshold of the church, a fine old woman who is lying in wait for me dashes before me and empties under my steps, in great handfuls, the contents of a basket of flowers. During this time, the young people climbing on the roof of the church set off the bells until it seems that they will demolish the building. This would not be difficult, for the church, a very old one, is constructed of earth, and I would not guarantee that the walls have held to the vertical. They have held up well, nevertheless, for I know not how long, thanks to the absence of humidity in the air and the scarcity of rain.[40]

While I prepare myself in the sacristy I hear Father Jean placing everyone in the church, giving his instructions in that stentorian voice with which he is gifted and which he no doubt owes to the pure air of the mountains of Auvergne where his youth unfolded. The air here on the Rio Grande, no less pure, has conserved it for him in all its fullness, and the Castilian vibrates on his lips in bursting notes like the trumpets of Jericho.

"Little girls to the right and little boys to the left, and nobody move!" says the voice, which wants to make itself gentle so as not to frighten, but which nails the youngsters in place.

Thanks no doubt to the thunderous effect of this Olympian organ, the long ceremony of the confirmation takes place this evening in relative calm.

It is not that the children do not appear struck by terror at my approach, as they did the day before in Las Cruces, but this is a mute terror. I hear distinctly the name that is to be given to each one confirmed, which Father Jean indicates to me as we move along.

These names that godfathers and godmothers choose for their godchildren are of a variety, a piety, and often of a remarkable originality.

There are those named Belén, Paz, Luz, Inés, Dolores, Beatriz, Incarnación, Trinidad, Navedad, Asunción, Carmen, Mercedes, Pilar, Soledad, Refugio, Guadalupe. Others receive names a little more singular: Concha [Concepción], Benita, Barbara, Artemisa, Chula [Gertrudes], Altagracia, Aurelia, Candelaria, Desideria, Eufemia, Erminia, Agapita, Gumersinda, Pastora, Esperanza, Serafina, Cleofas, Nemesia, Lazara, Benigna, Imelda, Tranquilina, Isaura, Apolonia, Griselda, Rosena. Here is, certainly, a catalog of names that are hardly common.

The names of men are no less foreign. They are named Espíritu, Primitivo, Braulio, Serapio, Angel, Leandro, Ruperto, Rosario, Reyes, Sacramento, Tiburcio, Santos, Porfiria, Patrocinio, Diego, Alonzo, Arnulfo, Juan de Dios, Homobono, etc.[41]

It requires great attention to carry off this calendar *sui generis* while performing the confirmation.

The ceremony is completed in good order, and each one returns to his home, perfectly happy.

VII

Towns of Arizona. Mexican hospitality. Customs of another time. The invaded civilization.

The sun begins to descend toward its setting. The hour is favorable for a tour of inspection. In order to return to the rectory, Father Jean and I make a long detour down the length of the shady roadways.

Since there exists no Commission of Public Streets, any more than of Roads and Bridges, in the Far West, the roads which serve as streets in La Mesilla are in a deplorable state. The great winds have piled up sand at certain points, and, two steps farther, have dug immense holes. But what is especially painful to see is the grass growing everywhere, giving these places the air of an abandoned village. Alas! This is only too true. La Mesilla, once the pearl of the valley, the rival of Las Cruces, is no more than a shadow of itself. Successive droughts, and the gradual diminishing of disposable water for irrigation, have thrown the population into misery, forcing a number of families to emigrate. Business has gone elsewhere. A large part of the fields stay fallow. Everywhere one sees closed up houses and abandoned gardens. The formerly numerous population is reduced to about 150 families, all Mexican, that is to say, all Catholic. These fine people live somehow or another, for better or worse, and the bad grows worse from day to day. And this is truly a great shame, for La Mesilla must have been a beautiful village.

The houses, all low (there is not a single house with a second story), are made of adobe.

Adobe is the Spanish name for the earthen brick, mixed with straw and dried in the sun, of which all Mexican villages are constructed. By way of a roof, a *torta*, or a flat roof made of mud, is laid on sprigs of straw and rests on a narrow trellis which serves as the ceiling. When a rainstorm soaks this coating, which is scarcely resistant, leaks appear everywhere and the house is inundated. When good weather returns, the owner climbs on his flat roof, applies a plaster of mud to the damaged spots, and all is well.

These houses of earth, hardly elegant, are without argument the best adapted to hot climates.[42] One finds them, it seems, in all South America, as, moreover, in Africa and in all the Middle East. Not costly, fire-proof, they offer sufficient shelter in a land where one lives mostly outdoors. Finally, they have the appreciable advantage of coolness in summer and warmth in winter, the adobe being a poor conductor of heat. Around the houses and down the length of the streets, cottonwoods, ash trees, arcwood trees, fig trees, and umbrella trees furnish abundant shade.

The umbrella tree (*Melia azedarach umbraculiformis*) is one of the most beautiful trees in this region.[43] It grows marvelously in the alkaline soils of Arizona. All it requires is water, in exchange for which it gives a luxurious foliage, rounded in the shape of an umbrella. The flowers, smaller than but resembling those of the lilac, give off a heady perfume in the springtime. The fruit, a round yellow berry, extremely hard, is, they say, a poison.

Across the village extend *acequias* [irrigation ditches] which bring the water of the Rio Grande to distribute among the properties. Too often they are empty for entire months, and this explains the present misery, for the life of the land depends on them.

In all its features, this village recalls in a striking fashion a small town of the Middle East. "Of sun, of silence, of walls of adobe, this is the Mexican village," according to a very accurate saying. With their mid-eastern physiognomy, these Mexican *pueblos* seem foreign in the United States, or, rather, one would not believe that he was still in America. This is Spain once more, the rural Spain of old, somewhat mixed with Anglo-Saxonism and a relic of Aztec survival.

Here again, one finds Spanish courtesy.

"What is your name?"

"*Pablo, Señor, a sus ordenes de Usted.*"

"Do you live here?"

"*Si, Señor*, here is my house; it is yours. Here are my horses, they are at your command."

"Ignorant as slaves and more courteous than princes," it has been said of these fine native peoples. And one may add, "Poor as crickets; hospitable as Croesus."

Mexican hospitality constitutes another similarity with the Middle East. The home is perhaps only a miserable hut, a *jacal*, there is inside perhaps only a crust of bread, and for sleeping, only an old sheepskin spread on the ground. No matter; all this is yours, the *jacal*, the crust, and the sheepskin.

"You are welcome here, *Señor*, in your own house."

And the masters of these places, without supping, will go peacefully to sleep outside with the chickens.

Contact with the whites, it is true, tends to make disappear, from day to day, this beautiful urbanity, completely natural and so gracious. The selfish manners of the "invader," as they call the American in their ballads, are not without a disturbing influence on the naturalness which formerly gifted the ancient inhabitants of these regions so well.

It was always thus. The race called "superior," that is to say, the most active, the most prosperous, the most powerful, leads the others in its ways. *Major pars trahit ad se minorem.* Unfortunately—and missionaries the world over are unanimous on this point—upon contact with the white race, the indigenous races almost always adopt its failings and ignore its virtues. From modern civilization they take scarcely more than the vices. This is the case in all the lands where the white has penetrated. And generally, unless the Catholic ethic comes to regenerate these contaminated races and save them from themselves, they disappear. Farewell, ancient virtues, sane and simple customs; farewell, noble and proud sentiments, unselfish life, calm and gentle. The age of gold replaces the golden age.

Thanks to the solid bonds which hold the Mexican populations to the aegis of the faith this evil has not yet ravaged these countrysides. The distance from cities has acted to preserve them. The *ranchero* still knows how to enjoy the charms of his rustic life. Surrounded by a numerous family, he seeks happiness in the domestic foyer. There he reigns in the manner of the patriarchs, honored and loved by all of his kin. The wife is the undisputed queen of the home.

Old age is the object of absolute respect and very special attentions. To smoke his *cigarillo* in the presence of his parents is a grave failing that a well-born son would never permit himself, even when he himself might be old enough to be the father of numerous children.

Someone told me the story of a young man from a good family, who by his talents had achieved the position of delegate from his province to the parliament in Washington. This young politician still had his father in his native land, and the latter learned with true sorrow that his son was going around, in the capital, neglecting his religious duties somewhat, to the point that he had omitted celebrating Easter that year.

Returning to his family during the vacation time, the delinquent found the author of his days filled with holy anger. On the spot, the indignant father, after a vehement reprimand, ordered his son to strip to the waist and administered a vigorous thrashing, accepted, moreover, with complete submission. This model of fathers, worthy of the time of Abraham, presents a heroic type which no doubt becomes rarer every day. But I could cite a number of features that attest to an admirable vigor of faith and strength of soul.

Whatever may be the weakening of character in the later generations, the old continue to provide an example of profound veneration for the priest. The minister of *Su Divina Majestad*, always welcome in the home, is treated with the greatest regard. The eagerness, the deference, the marks of confidence of which he is the object by these simple and good souls, who consider themselves highly honored by his visit, are the constant admiration of strangers passing through. Should he be called to a sickbed, all the neighborhood comes to kneel around. Should it be a matter of the last sacraments and holy water, pious hands take care to decorate the room, sweeping the dust, covering the walls with white hangings, preparing a small household altar by way of a temporary altar.

Death is gentle in these sympathetic surroundings, for it is always overwhelmed with attentions. Relations of all degrees, neighbors and acquaintances, make a rule of visiting the sick, of attending the dying. Each one helps, and contributes from what is his. Should a young mother leave this world, the *compadres* take on the task of raising the young family. Orphans always find those who will adopt them, and it is not rare to see large families grow indefinitely by the acquisition of new wards: one more mouth in the house, posh, is that all! The job is, moreover, singularly simplified by the completely natural lifestyle, naked of pretense, where false needs are rigorously excluded. In many homes poverty is great, but no Mexican ever dies of hunger. One lives from day to day, like the birds, without concern for the next day. The spartan frugality of these fine people equals their endurance and blunts the sense of deprivation, reducing the necessities of life for them to the most simple expression.

I have always thought, nevertheless, that despite the bucolic poetry of this kind of existence, it would be desirable for the Mexican Creole to resign himself less easily to his chronic poverty and seek to give himself and his family an honorable place in the sun.[44] Destitution passively accepted brings certain problems, and prolongs a servile condition without hope for improvement. Poverty honorably born is assuredly a very grand and beautiful virtue, but it can degenerate into a fault when it comes to disguise a core of indolence and a habit of incurable improvidence.

With energy, well-directed and sustained efforts, and a certain concern for the future, it is beyond any doubt that these children of nature, well-gifted moreover when it comes to the heart, would be able to leave conditions that somewhat resemble serfdom. They would be able to succeed, as the too rare exceptions demonstrate, in making themselves independent, in raising themselves a degree on the social ladder, and in playing a role less self-effacing and more deserving within the nation. It is not that the mestizo knows hopeless poverty, nor that in being less advantaged than others he feels himself diminished in his own eyes. No, as I have said, with the little that he has, he knows how to show himself as grandiose as a lord; and in his soiled, torn garments he maintains a proud carriage and sensitive character, just like the *hidalgos* of Navarre and Aragón. But in its own interest, out of sympathy for this noble and beautiful race, one cannot resist an immense desire to see it assert itself more, in the face of the somewhat haughty self-sufficiency of the newcomers who habitually and systematically despoil the lands of the ancient masters of the soil. Not a week goes by but that some domain, a patrimony left by ancestors, escapes from its earthly possessors to enlarge the fortune of some industrial entrepreneur of the white race. It is certainly irritating, for whoever has an honest soul and a belief in the eminent justice of things, to see the naive simplicity of this race of children shamefully exploited by the greed of heartless ones who are "Judaizing," and by the intrigue of unknown adventurers, and this under the cover of the law. Also, it is not rare to encounter, by chance, a handsome gentleman walking with head held high, his shirt front a constellation of diamonds and an enormous pendant of gold beating upon his chest, whom one had seen, several years before, arrive in the country dressed like a beggar, with all his fortune contained in a handkerchief at the end of a stick. Is it not the case, as the song says:

>We see the clerks
>   decked out
>Like princes
>Who came
>   naked
>From the countryside.

This is where we were with our sociological and philosophical thoughts when, the tour of the village completed, we returned to the rectory of La Mesilla.

VIII

⚱

The evening of a beautiful day. A gracious visit. Memories of sweet France. At the home of the Sisters of Mercy. On the way to San Miguel.

The final hours of the evening, when the tropical light begins to fade by imperceptible degrees, are always filled with charm. With good reason we compare the decline of a life passed nobly to the evening of a beautiful day.

Father Jean had left me alone at the lodging. While he attended to his business, with my breviary completed, I had all the leisure to admire one of those ravishing sunsets for which the wide open spaces of the Far West are justifiably famous.

Twilight has only a short duration in these parts. Night follows broad daylight almost without transition. In this pure and airy atmosphere, the horizon at sunset, very distant, appears illuminated over a vast expanse. Ethereal mists, which substitute for clouds in this rainless sky, rest in a halo which glows beyond the dark line of hills with a blinding luster. This is an incandescent cloth, a lake of gold, an ocean of fire, which stretches into infinite depths as you gaze. The great trees which rise here slash across this flaming setting the black masses of their powerful branches, while far away, very distant, lost in space, appears the shadow of some great bird, streaking with its heavy flight the luminous immensity that bathes the West.

At exactly the hour when the sun's glow is near extinction, a coolness is felt which glides over the earth like a beneficial emanation. At this moment, the temperature drops suddenly several degrees. A shiver of comfort permeates nature, as if it were exhausted by the pitiless heat from a sun never veiled during the long hours of the day. But often this caressing breeze is only momentary. When the purple has replaced the gold at sunset and night has fallen completely, the refreshing breath of the atmosphere often gives way, during the heart of the summer, to an absolute calm, and the first hours of the night are sometimes rather suffocating and heavy. But generally, on the high plains, this spasm is of short duration, and the night reclaims its rights, spreading over all that breathes a refreshing breeze that invites rest.

A gracious visit came to interrupt my contemplation. Little girls, knocking shyly at the entrance, were bringing me bouquets. It would be very difficult for me to enumerate the flowers that composed them, but certainly it had been necessary to ravage all the surrounding gardens to put together the voluminous spray of flowers. Not saying a word, their eyes sparkling with pleasure, with an important air and conscious of a serious duty fulfilled, they filled my arms with their fragrant harvest, and without awaiting my thanks, fled at top speed. The instant after, no doubt, out of breath and moved, they were telling their smiling mothers the happy result of their ambassadorship to the *Señor Obispo.*

Beautiful little souls, infinitely more beautiful than the flowers that your good little hearts offered me, may you grow always in beauty and in grace before the Lord, and age in your innocence without the breath of an evil world ever coming to tarnish it!

All good and simple natures love flowers: the Mexicans are wild about them; they love them no matter where, in old soap boxes, in cracked pots, in the remains of tin cans; they surround them with jealous care, and surely they would prefer to suffer from thirst themselves than to deny water to their favorite plants.

The little visitors had hardly left when Father Jean returned. This was the supper hour. After a modest meal, we went outside to the front of the house, and sat in the shadows resting and chatting for a long while before retiring. In the depths of this lost village two thousand leagues from our birthland, we talked of things of long ago, evoking a thousand memories of our distant homeland.

On all the shores in every part of the globe, at every hour, there are missionaries who cross paths. As soon as business is finished, conversation takes a sentimental turn; a word, a name returns suddenly to the lips: France, sweet France! There is so much to say, so many events to go over, so many impressions to exchange, and, finally, so many vows to formulate, that the subject, always reclaimed, always discussed, never wears out; when it is exhausted, one starts again. The most lengthy absence, the most eventful existence, under new skies, in foreign lands, never manages to erase in the soul of the missionary the image of his first land, the land in which he left the most beautiful days of his life, the best of his heart. How spiritedly, when they meet at the other end of the world, compatriots intone the immortal ballad of Chateaubriand:

> So many sweet memories have I
> Of the lovely place of my birth!
> My sister, how beautiful they were, those days—
>   —France!
> Oh, my country! Be my love
>   —always!

The day had risen perfectly pure and serene, as always, with a sky too invariably clear. This uniformity of a climate with weather that is always the same finally ends in tiring the soul, so true it is that "excess in anything is a shortcoming" and that variety is one of the elements of beauty.

So, under a sun already vivid despite the early morning hour, I set off again through the sandpits of the road to go to celebrate Mass in the little chapel at the convent of the Sisters of Mercy. These fine missionary Sisters, three in number, of whom one is housekeeper and the other two are school mistresses, teach the rudiments of knowledge to some one hundred Mexican children. A rather ornate room, furnished with an altar, serves them as a chapel. There they are, dividing their lives, obscure and peaceful, between prayer and apostleship through the school. My visit is a change, an event in their uneventful existence. I endeavor to fortify these good servants of the Lord by fatherly words of encouragement and call down, for them and for their work, all the blessings from on high.[45]

Returning to the rectory, we determine the program for the day. The rest of the morning will be devoted to preparations, and after the meal, toward 1:00, we will harness up and set out en route to the neighboring mission, the hamlet of San Miguel, located twenty-three kilometers down the valley from Mesilla. Upon our arrival, the bell will bring all the population to the church for the confirmation. We will spend the night at San Miguel, and the next day continue our journey, arriving around noon at the mission of La Mesa still further down the valley.

Lacking thrush, one settles for blackbirds, and lacking blackbirds, one settles for an omelet. That is what happened to us on that day, a Tuesday: lacking meat. Sufficiently fed nevertheless, we take our places with our baggage in Father Jean's buggy behind two solid horses. Father Jean takes the reins and we make our departure through the deserted streets, through the rows of empty, dilapidated houses. Soon the poor little village of La Mesilla disappears behind us in the cloud of dust raised by our vehicle.

For half an hour we proceed through the middle of cultivated fields. Then the vegetation suddenly ceases and we find ourselves in the brush. The sun, directly above us, makes itself felt vividly; the road, full of holes and dusty, makes the horses tug, but, as valiant animals accustomed to the country, they take us along at a good speed. At 4:00 we arrive at San Miguel, not having encountered a living soul and not having seen a single dwelling during this journey of twenty-three kilometers.

The New Mexico Portion of the Diocese of Tucson

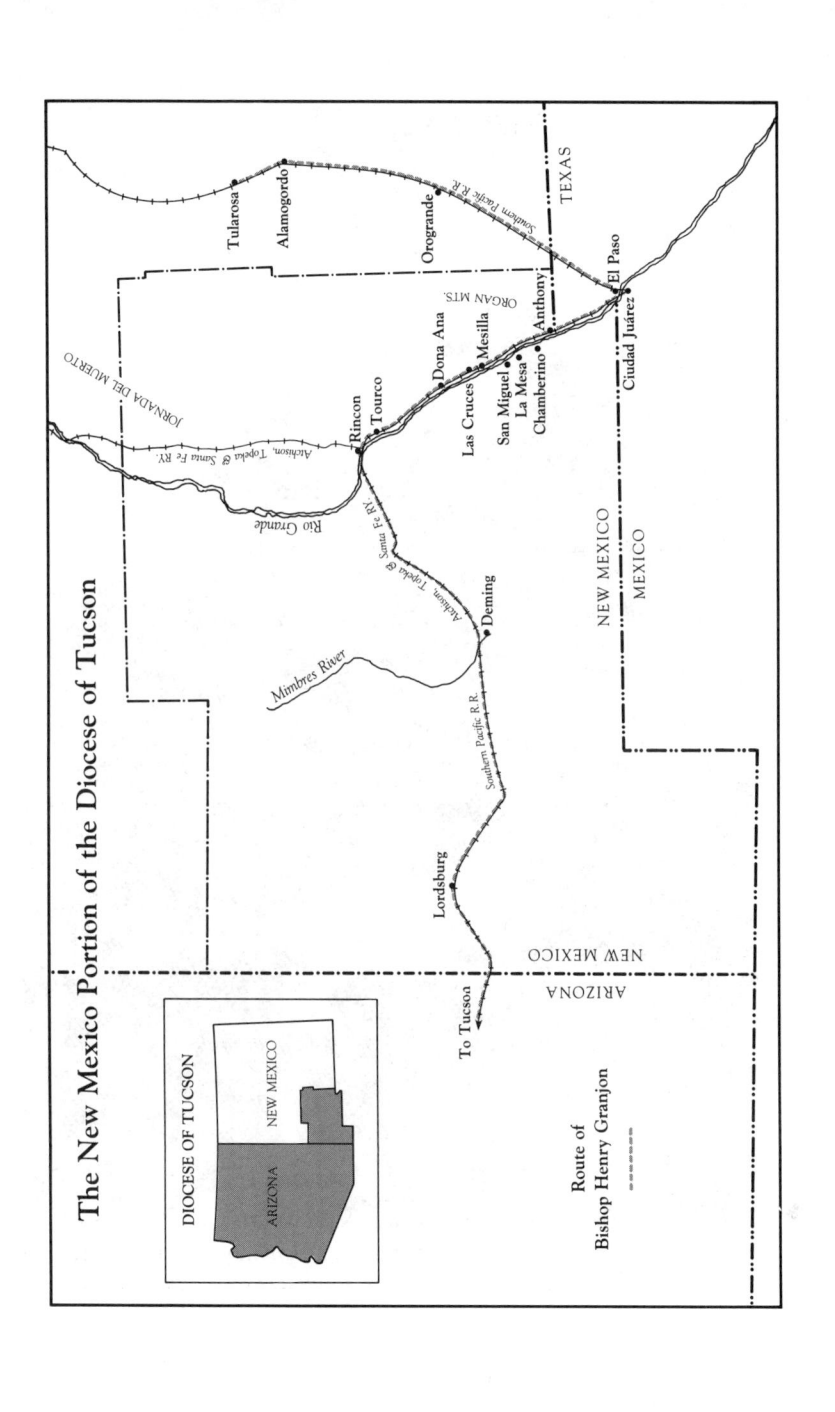

Route of
Bishop Henry Granjon

Bishop Henry Granjon at his work desk. (Courtesy Arizona Historical Foundation, Charles Trumbull Hayden University Library, Tempe, Arizona.)

Atchison, Topeka & Santa Fe Railway Station, Las Cruces, New Mexico, March 25, 1901. (Courtesy Rio Grande Historical Collections, New Mexico State University Library, Las Cruces.)

View of Las Cruces taken in 1903 from the second story of the Amador Hotel, looking north with St. Genevieve's Church in the background to the right. (Courtesy Rio Grande Historical Collections, New Mexico State University Library, Las Cruces.)

St. Geneviève's Church, Las Cruces, at the turn of the century. (Courtesy Rio Grande Historical Collections, New Mexico State University Library, Las Cruces.)

Loretto Academy, Las Cruces. (Courtesy Rio Grande Historical Collections, New Mexico State University Library, Las Cruces.)

San Albino Church, Mesilla, about the time of Granjon's visit. (Courtesy Rio Grande Historical Collections, New Mexico State University Library, Las Cruces.)

Calle Santiago looking west toward San Albino Church, Mesilla, about the turn of the century. (Courtesy Rio Grande Historical Collections, New Mexico State University Library, Las Cruces.)

An adobe church typical of those Granjon saw on his pastoral tour. This one is the Bosque Seco Church located approximately six miles south of Mesilla. It was not visited by Granjon. (Courtesy Rio Grande Historical Collections, New Mexico State University Library, Las Cruces.)

Interior of the Bosque Seco Church at the turn of the century. Note the vigas and the latilla ceiling. (Courtesy Rio Grande Historical Collections, New Mexico State University Library, Las Cruces.)

San José Church, La Mesa, in 1913. (Courtesy Rio Grande Historical Collections, New Mexico State University Library, Las Cruces.)

View of the *Acequia Madre*, Las Cruces, looking north toward the old Lucero Mill, 1891. (Courtesy Rio Grande Historical Collections, New Mexico State University Library, Las Cruces.)

Adobe houses in Tularosa, New Mexico, in October 1914. (Courtesy Rio Grande Historical Collections, New Mexico State University Library, Las Cruces.)

Collecting mesquite for firewood in the Mesilla Valley about the turn of the century. (Courtesy Rio Grande Historical Collections, New Mexico State University Library, Las Cruces.)

Jacal structure in Mesilla, about 1900. (Courtesy Rio Grande Historical Collections, New Mexico State University Library, Las Cruces.)

Rural Mesilla, about 1900. Note the adobe *hornos*. (Courtesy Rio Grande Historical Collections, New Mexico State University Library, Las Cruces.)

Family in front of an adobe house in the Mesilla Valley at the turn of the century. (Courtesy Rio Grande Historical Collections, New Mexico State University Library, Las Cruces.)

Construction typical of the early settlements in the area of old "Mesquite Lake" about ten miles south of Las Cruces. (Courtesy Rio Grande Historical Collections, New Mexico State University Library, Las Cruces.)

Placita, Thomas J. Bull's vineyard, Mesilla, July 21, 1897. (Courtesy Rio Grande Historical Collections, New Mexico State University Library, Las Cruces.)

View of Las Cruces and the Organ Mountains, 1930. (Courtesy Rio Grande Historical Collections, New Mexico State University Library, Las Cruces.)

IX

*San Miguel. En route. Don Perfecto. La Mesa;
its rectory and its church.*

San Miguel is a village of fifty families, living meagerly on the fruits of the land, lacking water to irrigate their plantings, and spending four-fifths of the year waiting for a rain that never comes.[46] Thus we find the population, free from any work in the fields, gathered around the church to receive us. Godparents and babies are ready for the confirmation. This takes place under the same uproarious conditions as during the preceding days.

Despite their poverty, the inhabitants of San Miguel have gone to some expense for the occasion. The interior of the small adobe church is all newly whitened; the earthen floor, which takes the place of flagstones or planks, has been carefully swept and then dampened to guard against the formation of dust by the trampling of the crowd. Neither chairs nor benches have hampered the operation, for one never sees seats in a Mexican church; the men stand, the women kneel on the ground. Curtains hang, freshly starched, at the clear glass windows. The altar disappears under a profusion of painted paper flowers, the product of local art, and above rises a beautiful statue of Saint Michael vanquishing the dragon, imported from France.

Each year, the day of the patron's festival, the archangel descends from his pedestal and is promenaded in a procession around the village. The crowd is so dense on these occasions that high mass and the vesper services must be celebrated outdoors. They raise a provisional altar on one side of the church. To protect heads from the heat of the sun, a *ramada* [canopy of greenery] is made out of cottonwood branches spread horizontally three meters from the ground. The posts that support this improvised roofing are still to be seen on the plaza, of which they take up a considerable portion.

The little room which is to serve as our lodging has been newly whitened also; the floorboards, or rather the earthen floor, have been carefully swept and dampened; two camp beds occupy the corners across from a large armoire. This is, quite simply, the sacristy, serving two needs. I sit on the edge of my bed and complete my breviary.

Then comes supper, which we take with a fine Mexican family that does us the honor of giving us the table during our brief stay.

Before night falls, we go to wander in the fields. These—alas!—lacking water, are almost all fallow. How is this poor village going to feed itself? Black misery is in sight for this year. The population, however, fatalistic in its ways and perfectly resigned, worries not at all about the future.

The night, in our dormitory-sacristy, was bad. Father Jean was suffering; air was lacking; I slept poorly.

So, at dawn we are up. I go out to say my prayers and to take some air. Already, saddled horses are at the tethering pole on the plaza. The *rancheros*, living far away, have not waited for daylight to come to the church. Filled with people, large wagons pulled by lean animals are arriving from all directions.

Soon there is great animation in this normally sad and silent hamlet. The church fills, and mass is celebrated before the statue of the prince of the heavenly militia that these good people never tire of admiring.

The distance from San Miguel to La Mesa is only five kilometers. The road traverses cultivated fields, all more or less withered. In many places, the brush has reclaimed possession of the earth; the vegetation is dead from thirst.

This time we have an escort. A horseman trots before us as a vanguard. He is an old man of seventy-two years who answers to the name of Don Perfecto. He came early this morning to meet us at San Miguel, from the depths of some retreat lost in the valley, for the sole purpose of greeting "His Lordship," attending the services, and accompanying us to La Mesa.

Don Perfecto is a Mexican half-breed of the old school, of the best type. His adventurous life, in the distant years of his youth, during the time of the Mexican civil wars and the era when all the region became the territory of the Republic of the United States, was replete with dazzling feats. He is the size of a giant, his face swarthy, his eyes dark and ardent. His carriage is proud, but in the presence of the *Padre* and of *Su Illustrisima*, he is very humble and very noble, of exquisite courtesy. Until old age first touched him, his existence was, they say, a rather stormy one. But already, for many years now, he has edified all the countryside by his exemplary piety. Father Jean, who esteems him highly, tells me that he is a very devout man. Often, during the time of the great floods of the Rio Grande, he transported the missionary and his baggage across the tumultuous waters of the river by swimming. Taming the wild horses of the prairie was always his favorite occupation. As a young man, what a magnificent horseman he must have made!

I see him several meters ahead, straight as a lance on his frisky mustang, as one with his mount, and circling, despite his years, with an admirable elegance, indicating to us with a noble gesture the potholes to go around and the best routes to take.

All by himself he makes a complete escort, and were it not for the evident poverty of his clothing, he could pass for a huntsman in a prince's household. One thing intrigues me: atop the tatters of his lamentable costume he wears a bowler hat, descending to his ears, of which he is obviously very proud, to judge from the minute attentions that he squanders on it. I ask the Father:

"Where was he able to hunt out that unlikely felt hat?"

"That," Father Jean answers me, "is an old hat that I brought from France an incalculable number of years ago, and that I gave to him years ago. The gentleman decks himself out in it for great occasions. . . ."

I note with pride this magnificent proof of the incontestable superiority that marks the products of French industry. Assuredly a headcovering imported from Chicago had not before had such a hard life. Oh, where patriotic vanity lodges itself! I had come, making our way along the road, to follow with affection this poor, collapsed felt hat which filled me with the same respect that warriors of yesteryear reserved for the white plumes of Henry the Fourth.

At 10:30 the felt hat of Don Pedro makes a half turn, and our noble escort indicates to us with a gesture and a glance the outskirts of the hamlet of La Mesa.[47] Several minutes later, the horses stop before a large back door with worm-eaten panels, lopsided and loose. This is the rectory, but all in ruins. Such as it is, it nevertheless has on us the effect of a palace of delights. In these large chambers, where we will lodge for twenty-four hours, coolness awaits us, tranquility and rest, and also meditation. We are on the eve of the Ascension, and it is now a matter of preparing properly for the celebration.

Immediately upon our arrival, I visit the church.[48] It rises massive and heavy (the walls are four to five feet thick) on the other side of the road, at the far end of a large space which in former times was the plaza. The Mexicans always give their religious buildings the place of honor, on the plaza, in the heart of the city or village. No hamlet, moreover, as miniscule as it may be, is without its plaza; the Americans, in the laying out of their cities, have not followed this example. This is a mistake, in my opinion. But we must remember that, with regard to the motto *"Utile dulci,"* the Americans appreciate and practice only the first term. The artistic side of things leaves them indifferent. Their conception of life is quite different.

The church is of adobe, without flooring, and with a flat roof. It dates from long ago, from the time when this region was part of the Diocese of Durango, in Mexico.

There was then a priest living in La Mesa, the center of the parish: this explains the presence of an old rectory in this lost corner of the world. The altar, the work of Father Jean, like all the furniture of the church and sacristy, is of wood, unpainted, but remarkably preserved by the dryness of the atmosphere.

I note that the inhabitants, on the occasion of this pastoral visit, have underpinned all the walls at the base and have inserted a bedrock of stones—an indispensable operation, for the old walls are beginning to lean in a disturbing fashion. Buttresses also have been built up on the side of the church that faces the river, the latter, although several miles distant, being a perpetual menace. Several years ago, the Rio Grande, in one of its terrible overflowings, advanced its waters clear to the church and barely failed to carry it off.

Around the church, on the edge of the plaza, rows of immense cottonwoods present soaring profiles against a distant sky, where not a single ramshackle dwelling, not a single obstacle, interrupts the view of the vast, concave expanse. A few low houses, quite far off, can barely be seen.

In this magnificent solitude, in the middle of this grandiose forest, in the silence of these almost uninhabited places, the old church has the effect of a solitary, ancient temple surviving the generations that have passed away. Not a voice is heard, not a being moves in the vast and deserted plaza. Without the splendid light that falls from the constantly shining sun and that gives the feeling of a perpetual festival to the mute, immobile scene, the impression would be sad, agonizing, like a great abandoned cemetery.

X

Confirmation at La Mesa. The peanut vendor and his donkey. Through fields. Beautiful and poetic evening.

At noon a mestizo comes to get us and guide us to his residence, where dinner is awaiting us.

Great preparations have been made in my honor. The room where we enter, converted into a dining room, is joyful to see: everything here is blazing new. The master of the house has, "as poorly as well," covered the walls with wallpaper. A roller must have been lacking, for one sees here and there cracks covered with diverse fragments. This mixture, however, does not displease him; on the contrary, the fine man is full of pride in his work and supremely happy to do us the honors of his house.

On a small round table in the middle of the room are placed brand-new tin utensils, recently bought in town. In the Spanish style, a cup of chocolate begins the meal. Poultry, accompanied by corn, beans, and rice, constitutes the menu; all is washed down with large glasses of water and coffee.

While we eat, the lady of the house, armed with a towel, busies herself, without a moment of respite, in chasing flies from the table. It is simple, without formality, but in its naive form this hospitality is generous and touching.

Beginning at 1:00, a little life begins to reappear around the lonely church. Some carts arrive. Babies begin to fill the air with their vigorous protests.

At 3:00 the confirmation ceremony takes place. Then we

dismiss the congregation, since most of the people live far away and are obliged to return home for the night. We take care to warn them to return the following morning, without fail, for the Feast of the Ascension and to attend Mass.

Soon the large, deserted plaza and the silent hamlet, shaken for a moment from their torpor by this short-lived gathering, fall once more into their customary silence.

In the shadow of the great walls of the church there remains no person other than a small, lame man, standing near a small donkey of an odd appearance, which dozes tranquilly between the shafts of a miniscule cart of unlikely form. I had already noticed this bizarre couple when we stopped at San Miguel. Donkey-driver and cart have followed us on our pastoral pilgrimage. The good man sleeps at night between the wheels of his vehicle, and during the day attends to his little business, which consists of selling peanuts.

By this singular name are known the fruits of a leguminous plant called, I believe, by the learned name of *Arachis hypogoea*. They ripen in the earth and consist of a shell enclosing one or two nuts, which, when browned, have a flavor that is highly agreeable *sui generis*. This is a tidbit for all children, large and small.

The peanut vendor obviously has not accumulated a great fortune from his humble occupation. His outlay is more than simple: his cart, made of old boards, apparently borrowed from packing crates from Chicago, rolls on two bowed wheels. But his donkey merits, by itself, an entirely individual study. It appears to belong to a unique species: its ears, instead of standing up straight, sometimes unfurl like a fan of feathers, and sometimes hit its cheeks like a cat-o'-nine-tails. Personal and minute observations reveal the cause of this droll peculiarity: multiple cuts have been made in the ears of the poor young donkey, and these gashes have left a multitude of thin strips of leather which, from a distance, give the animal an extraordinary appearance. Some sorry wag must have perpetrated this crime one night in the moonlight while the owner slept the sleep of the just under his vehicle.

Whatever may be made of this final point, the vendor seems a joyful fellow, of invariable and exuberant gaiety. He is the most popular man in the region. He possesses the secret of amusing children, and since, moreover, he is totally inoffensive, he has free access everywhere, and is part of every festival.

A poet, he improvises compliments in verse, on the spot, and makes up impromptu songs that are always appropriate. Here is one who scarcely feels the weight of misery! Possibly, underneath it all, he is one of those stoic philosophers such as one finds, often enough, among the most humble Mexicans. It is certain that his religious sentiments contribute to maintaining serenity within his soul.

Passing before our door, he stops to greet us graciously, and from the bottom of his rolling box he takes out two oranges, the only ones he has, no doubt, and offers them to us with the happiest and most amiable of smiles.

We have decided, Father Jean and I, to hurry up supper and to spend the last hour of the day going across the countryside. We walk at random, straight ahead, among parched lands, abandoned and uncultivated, but which, revived by irrigation, would be admirably fertile. A square plot on the edge of the road is completely covered by six pear trees of enormous dimension, the largest that I have ever seen, planted there some thirty years ago. Their roots, no doubt, reach humid depths whence they can defy the persistent droughts. Everywhere the surface soil shows itself full of good intentions and awaiting only that vital and indispensable element, water, to revive its latent fecundity and cover itself with profitable growth. Grasses, less delicate but useless, grow in total aridity. It is a distressing sight. Only the large trees, with roots deeply established in the earth, resist this implacable sky of bronze; they spread over the inert, fallow lands the wasted benefit of their shade.

There is, in front of the rectory, a row of umbrella-trees, very old, very large, with leaves scarcely visible but covered with clusters of flowers the color of lilacs. Their fragrance, concentrated like a perfume by virtue of the arid soil, saturates the surrounding air, oppressing the sense of smell to the point of nausea. Fortunately, a wind comes up at bedtime which dissipates these far too heady emanations. The wind blows in great gusts during the first hours of the night, reproducing outside, through the masses of great cottonwoods on the plaza, the roaring of stormy seas. Then the hurricane calms, and, before I succeed in falling asleep, the air becomes absolutely calm.

From my open window, while awaiting stubborn sleep, I watch the thick foliage of the plaza become suddenly still. All around the profound darkness which falls from the giant trees, the sky, twinkling with stars, lavishes that sublunary twilight which bathes regions with very dry, hot climates like phosphorescent light. The small adobe church appears massive, inordinately enlarged, in the surrounding chiaroscuro.

The transparency of the air is so great that, beyond the emptiness of the plaza, one can see, stretching to infinity in the direction of the south, for the length of the valley, the high branches of cottonwoods, very distant, lost in the solitude. Over all this sleeping nature hovers a silence of nothingness, immense and unfathomable as that on high, in the depths of the sidereal world.

From the depths of this peaceful, silent night, distant chords are heard. These are the plaintive sounds of a Spanish guitar. Arpeggios, a light prelude, then the voice of a woman, fresh and smooth, the range attenuated by the distance. The song reaches me only as a faint echo. But from the first measures I recognize *La Golondrina* [The Swallow], that ballad so popular in Spain and in all of Latin America, whose melancholy and sentimental inspiration corresponds so well to the Spanish soul. The melody is sad and languid; the words are filled with emotion:

> A donde irá, veloz y fatigada
> La Golondrina que de acquí se va?
> Mas si en el campo andurà extraviada,
> Buscando abrigo, y no lo encontrarà!
>
> Junto a mi lecho le pondré su nido,
> En donde pueda la estación pasar . . .
> También yo estoy en la región perdido . . .
> ¡Oh! ¡Cielo santo! ¡Y sin poder volar!⁴⁹

In the nocturnal silence of solitude, this distant voice has something mystical; this sweet, disconsolate song crosses the air shivering, as in a celestial lament.

During this evening of religious ceremony, some innocent, pure soul had tasted happiness, and before sleep came to cause it to fade away, it had wanted to send forth its dreamy joy.

Religious melancholy is one of the traits of the Spanish disposition. Catholic Spain, which came to evangelize these regions during the great ages of faith, brought into the hearts of the neophytes the taste for spiritual and divine things, the mysticism which penetrates its own spirit and which shapes, in the New World, the souls of ascetics. The breath of the modern spirit has tarnished, alas!, the splendor of this moral beauty, which for a long time was the superlative spiritual binding of the societies of Latin America. There are still many remnants, however. In simple natures, those which the contagion of the century has not affected, the Christian conception of life, or the "Catholic sense," has remained intact; faith holds firm in all its grace. On the slope of a hill, a peasant from the mountains of Mexico has raised a humble burial monument, and the passer-by can read, touched and moved, this sublime epitaph:

> TO THE MEMORY
> OF MY CHERISHED WIFE.
> SHE HAS LEFT ME
> LEAVING IN MY HEART THE PAIN
> FROM WHICH SHE SUFFERED
> AND FROM WHICH SHE DIED:
> THE LONGING FOR THE CELESTIAL HOMELAND.

XI

The feast of the Ascension. Enroute to Chamberino. Touching and solemn reception. A bishop without mitre or cross.

There was at La Mesa, they tell me, in days of old, a flourishing town, populous and full of life. Persistent drought provoked emigration. Deserted houses have fallen, little by little, into ruins. The population has dispersed throughout the valley. In the afternoon, we see the remaining families arriving from all sides and converging on the church for the confirmation. A dozen families have resisted the contagion of discouragement which depopulated this beautiful town; their houses and the plantings bordering them make the picture somewhat more cheerful and save it from a sense of absolute desolation.

In the rectory, two spacious, high-ceilinged rooms are occupied for one day each month. The other rooms are either totally in ruins, with the roofs giving way, or else they are in a state of complete decrepitude and almost uninhabitable. I cannot resist a feeling of melancholy in the presence of all these things which palpitated with life in the wonderful days of yesteryear, and from which life continues to retreat, awaiting complete abandonment. Ruins always sadden the soul, which, remembering its origin, aspires to eternity in all things.

On the day of the Ascension, holy Mass is celebrated early in the morning. Breakfast is eaten in haste at the home of my Mexican host. I walk, then, in leisurely fashion around the plaza, inhaling the morning's freshness under the great green domes of the cottonwoods.

The sun has risen, as usual, as always, in a sky without clouds. Another hot day announces itself, as there have been hot days for months without respite. To crown the joy of this feast day a rain would be necessary, one of those all too rare summer rains which save this country from complete desolation. But there will be nothing, assuredly; rainstorms are a long time in forming, and they always announce themselves several days in advance.

Two bells ring loud and clear. I look toward the church and see Father Jean mounted on the flat roof, sounding the carillon with his hands, each armed with an end of rope. This is the first part of the parish Mass, which will be followed by a final ceremony of confirmation. Slowly, the carriages arrive, making good speed in the fresh air.

At the moment when Father Jean begins Mass, the church is filled. I see Don Perfecto in a corner very close to the altar, kneeling on the earth, his hands joined, meditative and pious as an angel. His hat is placed next to him, and he surveys it with solicitude, fearing an accident in the congestion of the crowd. The kneeling women, surrounded by children, cross themselves frequently in the Spanish way, kissing their thumbs after each sign of the cross.

The offices have ended, very simply, without any possibility of solemnity, since the elements to bring out the luster of the ceremonies are lacking. It is even difficult to find lay brothers for Mass. The missionary serves all functions: those of bell ringer, sexton, choirboy, etc.

They even tell of an old missionary, with a turn of spirit more ingenious than liturgic who dreamed up the idea of attaching a bell to his heel, in order to compensate for the lack of an altar boy. The bell rang at the customary moments during the course of the Mass, and the good mestizos, not at all offended, would redouble their attention and fervor.

An hour afterwards, the last lingerers again take up the road to their *rancherías*, and the plaza falls once more into its mournful, vast, and sunlit solitude.

This day finishes my visit to the district served by Father Jean. At the sound of midday, the R.P. Jesuit charged with the missions of Chamberino and Anthony comes to lead me lower down the valley for a visit with his flock.[50]

At the designated hour, the Father arrives with military exactitude. There is something of the soldier in Father L. Born in Bordeaux, and now in the full strength of his years, small in size but muscled and vigorous, he has the demeanor of a cavalry officer. I see him arrive, head covered by an immense Mexican *sombrero*, skin tanned,[51] white with dust from head to foot. Out of respect, he has come to get me in a carriage, but his favorite means of locomotion is invariably by horseback. He has two saddle horses. Every two or three years he has to replace them; his horseback trips by night and day have finished them, worn them out. He is the ardent, never-tiring kind of missionary.

We all dine together, and toward 1:00 we get on the road to Chamberino.

Father Jean conducts us half way, to the limit of his district. The distance to travel is only thirteen kilometers. We will arrive at 3:00. The country is low; everywhere there are alluvial lands. The soil, less dry, is covered in places with plants, and our route passes through a thicket of underbrush. But houses and farms are thinly sown. These are still immense stretches that are uninhabited, deserted. The scarcely frequented roads allow themselves to be invaded by shoots of mesquite which obstruct passage and whip one in the face, if one is not careful to defend oneself by raising an arm at eye level.

The mesquite (*Prosopis pubescens*) grows wild, and is rather prevalent in these regions of the Southwest; its presence always indicates good land. The knotty, tortured, and extremely hard wood is used almost entirely for firewood. Nevertheless, the old trunks of those trees which have been allowed to reach full growth form excellent beams, dark red and very heavy, which defy the centuries.

We arrive at an arroyo. This is the limit of the district. Father Jean bids farewell to us, and retraces his steps by the trot of his two horses.

On the other side of the arroyo the solitude is peopled; there is great animation. The people of Chamberino—men, women, and children, in their Sunday best and joyous—have come to meet us. Wagons whose axle trees cry out under their loads fall in behind us, one after another, on the narrow road, raising a whirlwind of dust. As we advance, other carts emerge from all sides and take their place in the procession. Everyone is outside, and Father L. exults. His flock has been faithful to his order. At a curve in the road he invites me to look behind us. The line of wagons extends as far as the eye can see, half lost in the cloud of dust.

A little farther ahead, two arches of green rise in the middle of the road, leaving just enough room to pass underneath.

At the moment that we pass under the arches, at a walk, as is proper, an old woman advances before the horses and scatters on the ground the contents of a basket of flowers.

At the same instant we see, coming from afar, an old man, hobbling along. It is, no doubt, the worthy spouse of the venerable florist. He pushes, laboriously, a wheelbarrow loaded with a barrel. Evidently he is straining to arrive on time. Father L. explains to me that it is a barrel of water, which the good old man would like to spread along our passage to keep down the dust. He does not arrive in time, and I am distressed not to have been aware of the old man's project sooner. We would have halted rather than allowing him to miss his move.

Fine people! But also, fine and holy missionary: *forma facti gregis ex animo.*

Several more kilometers, and there, on the flank of the hill, rises the silhouette of the little chapel of Chamberino.[52] We arrive at the foot of the knoll. We set foot to earth, and, under a veritable tunnel of greenery, of branches of tamarinds, pricked by Castilian roses, we advance majestically toward the church, while over the door a young fellow astride the roof rings the bells with all his strength.

This entry under the bursting sun of 3:00, followed by this royal cortege, among the greenery and the flowers, is something grandiose . . . for the region. Everything is relative in this world. I have only the time to hurry to the sacristy to change from my traveling costume into my official dress.

The crowd has invaded the church, and they are awaiting, with a few words of greeting, a first pastoral blessing. Moved, I express to these good children of nature all the satisfaction with which their superb reception has filled me, praying to God to receive their goodwill kindly and to repay it a hundredfold. I announce that the evening confirmation will be given at 4:00, and that in the evening there will be rosary prayers and benediction and the holy sacrament. The congregation leaves the chapel in great happiness.

There is a shadow over their contentment, however. Father L. confides it to me discreetly. A bishop with neither mitre nor cross is, for them, only half a bishop, and since I must reduce my baggage to the strict minimum for these visits "of long passage," the simplicity of my attire has grieved them.

Facing the truth of these assertions, I resolve to procure for myself a small, light mitre and an aluminum cross, collapsible and transportable. And my good flock of Chamberino, so cordial and generous, will not experience in the future the disappointment that afflicts them today.

XII

⚱

*Confirmation at Chamberino. Don Pancho.
En route to Anthony. A princely gift.*

At 4:00 everything is ready; godfathers and godchildren are gathered at the church. The brouhaha begins as usual: a concert of tears in unison, enraged cries of *enfants terribles*, agitation of parents, confusion all down the line. Finally the ceremony is completed, and large and small hasten to leave from the too-narrow confines and go out into the open air to compose themselves.

The chapel, in fact, is very small, of dried earthen brick, and all alone on its hill, whence the eye embraces an immense panorama.

This part of the valley is green, lower, no doubt, and a little less dry than the part at La Mesa. Near the chapel, the hamlet is made up of three houses in all, or, rather, one house and two small cabins of earth with corrals, or circular enclosures, in which to keep the livestock. The house is a gathering point. The population from several leagues around converges here on the day when the missionary comes to make his monthly visit.

Within the house, the proprietor, an aged Mexican and a devout Catholic, has prepared hospitably for me. The large room is assigned to me, and all his family crowds together, somehow or another, in the only bedroom that remains. There are grapevines around, for I see on the table in my apartment a decanter of red wine flanked by a jug of water, and my host amiably invites me to refresh myself. Then we chat. The friends of the household come to greet me.

Father L. is slow in coming to sup. I look for a book, a brochure, anything to occupy my attention, but I search in vain. However, my host has understood: from the bottom of a large trunk which comprises almost all of the furniture, he takes out a book of prayer written in the purest Castilian, and I do my reading.

As the night is falling, we meet at the church for the devotionals of the month of Mary. Attendance is high: not a soul misses the call.

Father L. takes up the word and addresses an eloquent sermon to the attentive group. The Spanish language lends itself marvelously to the development of oratory, to movements of pathos. This is a language eminently Christian, greatly superior in this regard to English. Father L. greatly desires to profit from the occasion of my visit by bringing back to the sacraments several recalcitrants who have strayed from the flock, and he has chosen death as the subject of his discourse. His sermon bears fruit, to judge from the great number of men who come afterwards, one after another, to find me in the back of the little sacristy.

Also, the next morning at mass, communions are numerous and attendance at a maximum. Some of the faithful have spent the night there, sleeping under the stars.

Today we must cross the Rio Grande and arrive in the afternoon at Anthony for the confirmation. Anthony is located lower down the valley, about ten kilometers from Chamberino.
Father L. gives his orders for departure toward the middle of the day. Thus we have an entire morning to ourselves. I profit from this by making a tour of the cultivated fields. Don Pancho serves me as guide. He has me mount his little cabriolet and leads me to see his properties.

Don Pancho is the great landowner of this part of the valley, which is explained by the fact that he is completely Americanized and gets along well in business matters. We arrive at his vineyards, very well kept, very flourishing. Farther away are vast fields of alfalfa. A few tamarinds can be seen in all directions.[53] Around the house there is an orchard. At some distance, Don Pancho points out to us an old cemetery. This is a large square invaded by thick brush from which protrudes, here and there, the debris of wooden tombstone crosses. This cemetery has had to be abandoned. Some time ago, the Rio Grande, which passed by some three kilometers from there, submerged these lands in a sudden flood. One may glimpse, through the thick undergrowth, the ruins of the former church of the mission, which also had to be abandoned for the same reason.

Meanwhile, Father L. rejoins us on horseback, as is customary. Don Pancho does us the honors of his house. The living room offers a certain luxury, for here is an old piano, and, on a small round table, a family album.

Above the door I notice a large glassed-in frame. Upon inspection, it reveals itself to be one of those souvenirs of marriage in the form of a painting containing relics. In the center, a photograph: Don Pancho and his young wife in wedding garb. All around, the white veil of the bride, garlands of artificial orange blossoms, and below—singular idea!—the two satin shoes worn by the young Mexican woman on the great day of the wedding.

At the midday meal, Don Pancho has us taste the wine of the region, which is awful but at least has the advantage of being absolutely natural.[54]

The hour of departure approaches. Wagons arrive filled with people for escort. A troop of horsemen takes off at a gallop. The signal is given at 1:30. The covered carriage which carries Father L. and me begins the march. Through the fields we mark out a road to reach the Rio Grande. Trees and tall brush abound, and the branches lash our faces in passing. The column descends in good order toward the bed of the river, which we reach in half an hour.

The Rio Grande is completely dry, indicated only by sands in a large depression in the soil. The river is the demarcation between Chamberino and Anthony, our objective. The escort stops at the edge and allows us to cross the river bed alone. On the other bank, at the exact place where we will go to reascend the steep bank of the river, an arch of greenery is raised. The people of Anthony are there, in wagons, on horseback, covering the embankment. We pass under the arch and soon are forced to stop. The crowd comes to greet us and kiss my ring. They all file up, hurrying, jostling, but without a sound, in a religious silence. The people of Chamberino, on the other side of the river, await a final farewell benediction, which I send them by a high, grand gesture. Then they turn back to return to their homes.

We regroup then, in a column. The horsemen, a whole squadron, take their place behind my wagon. The small wagons follow in single file.

There remain six or seven kilometers to cross. The road, full of holes, pulverized by months of drought, is a bed of grey dust where the horses sink to their knees. The wheels dig a furrow while kicking up a cloud of fine powder, added to by the cavalcade that gambols behind us. At the same time, the sun sends forth its burning rays, which put us in a sweat. We pass under other arches of greenery planted right in the middle of the road, appearing everywhere that signs of habitation can be seen. A great dead snake, hanging from a tree branch, brushes our faces as we pass. The dust becomes blinding. Finally, at a bend in the road, we glimpse Anthony, that is to say, three or four houses of adobe of which one serves for the moment as chapel. It is around 3:00 and the heat is so intense, the dust so thick, that the first thing to do upon arrival obviously is to search for a retreat and from here to proceed to a complete cleaning. The operation is made easier for me by the intelligent attentions of a good old "mother" who grasps the situation at first sight, conducts me to a house with great politeness, sends out for a brush, calls for a bucket of water and towels, and installs me in the dwelling. This is the residence of her son, recently married, and this is to be my house during the time I spend in Anthony, the key having been given over to me and the young couple having gone, very graciously, to install themselves elsewhere. Here, certainly, is hospitality as of old![55]

"*Cleanliness next to saintliness*" say the Americans. [First saintliness, then cleanliness.] That afternoon, this principle, which conforms perfectly to the requisites of hygiene, has no partisan more convinced than I. Given the varnish made of dust and sweat which covers me from head to feet, I do not remember ever having appreciated more, in my diverse peregrinations, this precious gift of nature: water. It is necessary to have lived in these arid regions, in the plains of dust and the deserts of thirst, truly to understand the magic of this word: water, water.

My *toilette* completed, I am a new man, fresh and fit, ready to give audience with the most amiable grace. I open my door to eager visitors. One of them is a venerable old man by the name of Cecilio Jiménes, who, after the customary greetings, puts between my hands, without saying a word, a carefully wrapped document. I open it. It is a notarized act, in good and correct form, transferring to the bishop of Arizona and to his successors the ownership of a large square of land situated in these places, as a donation, to be used for the erection of a chapel in the name of Saint Isidore. This is a princely gift on the part of this man, who is manifestly poor. In the name of the Church, I thank him effusively, calling down all the blessings of Heaven upon him. Calm and modest, he refuses the thanks, only too happy to divest himself for the glory of God, and finding his generous act the most natural thing in the world. "*Sea por Dios!*" he says simply, upon retiring. I promise myself to visit him, in his simple mestizo peasant's home, before leaving Anthony.

During this time the preparations for the confirmation have been completed, and I take myself, at 4:00, to the locale which serves as a chapel. I find there a small ramshackle house of earth, of the most primitive kind, absolutely crammed with people.

The confirmation ceremony is very laborious this time. The atmosphere, saturated with dust and suffocating with heat, overstimulates the crowd, and the children stamp their feet. It is necessary to dry their heads, which are drenched with sweat, to receive the holy water. I have to forego circulating among the rows; this is impossible. A pin could not fall to the ground. I establish myself in front of the altar, and want the godparents and godchildren to file before me. But the crowding is so great that these poor people, squeezed as if in a keg of anchovies, are not able to reach me except by dint of a thousand persistent efforts. And over all this heat, over this teeming, suffocating crowd, the enraged cries soar above, emerging without respite from the little gullets of 150 exasperated children.

However, thanks to patience, calm, and method, we come to the end. Ouf! What relief to go outdoors into the open air! The men wipe their brows with the backs of their hands; and right away, to comfort themselves, roll between thumb and index finger a small corn-husk *cigarillo* in the Mexican style. As for the poor mothers, whom I pity with all my heart, they all bear up without a complaint, smiling, even happy, and overjoyed once the ceremony is completed, in proportion to the degree of pain endured.

Obviously, a little church is necessary for Anthony; a mission chapel is in order, sufficiently large to hold all these people on the days of great abundance. These fine people acknowledge this themselves, and on the land donated by Cecilio Jiménes, they have begun to lay the first foundations for a chapel of adobe. Only, whether because of lack of resources to proceed, or lack of water to soften the earth for adobes, the work has been suspended.

After supper, I visit Don Cecilio Jiménes and his worthy wife. The two old people inhabit a hut of earth in the shadow of vast cottonwoods. Everything is poor, primitive. This is the ancient simplicity. They have grown old here, in calm and solitude, ignorant of cities and the modern world, content with little, living in the open air. And this sweet, peaceful existence has fashioned them in its image: everything breathes serene tranquility both in their persons and in the things that surround them. I believed I saw Philemon and Baucis, those two Phrygians of mythology, who, in recompense for the hospitality they offered to Jupiter and Mercury when they came disguised, saw their simple home transformed into a magnificent temple and they themselves metamorphized into flowering lime trees before the door of the temple. This is indeed such a case. My two friends, upon the visit of their bishop, have generously offered the most beautiful portion of their domain to build a temple to the Lord. Their mortal remains no doubt will rest in the shadow of this sanctuary; and one day, transfigured in glory, they will be reborn to life, their brows crowned, holding in their hands before the throne of the Eternal One the palms of triumph.

The bell announces the hour of the exercises of the month of Mary; night falls gently, calming all this nature which has been distraught with sun and heat. And with the freshness of the evening a great silence, solemn and profound, descends on the valley. The high branches cease to rustle. The crickets strike up their nocturnal song on all sides. And in the peace of this corner of the world, lost and solitary, young voices rise, singing hymns to the Blessed Virgin.

These innocent voices, rising in the tranquil air of the night, harmonize with the impression of pious melancholy reflected on all these open faces at this mysterious hour when nature hushes and sleeps. They seem, among these simple souls gently resigned to their life of misery in this valley of tears, like an echo of distant happiness, a memory of Eden. *Ad te clamamus exules. . . . Ad te suspiramus, gementes et flentes, in hac lacrymarum valle. . . .*

The genius of the Castilian tongue lends itself admirably to the expression of delicate and profound feelings.

If, as the song affirms:

> In former times, your Majesty,
> Arabia, in fleeing from you
> Left on your queenly brow
> Its crown of the East;

the Spanish soul and its language have also kept the East's vivacity of passions, richness of imagination, image-filled and flowery speech, and ardent and deep feeling.

These poetic expressions of piety are sung in airs unique, unimaginable, and completely foreign to the modern style. This music, sentimental and expressive, well-adapted to the words, has something of the archaic, of the mozarabic perhaps; moreover, a very great number of expressions in the Spanish vocabulary date entirely from the time of the Moors.

The following day, Saturday, May 10, we arise "at the crow of the rooster," although here this expression lacks accuracy since the roosters crow all through the night.

This will be our last day on the banks of the Rio Grande. In the morning, I am to go to the Santa Fe railroad station of La Tuna, three miles from Anthony, and from there reach the city of El Paso in Texas. Then, at 8:00 in the evening, a train of the Rock Island line will take me northeast as far as the foot of the Sierra Sacramento where the villages of Tularosa and Alamogordo, the last two stops of my pastoral tour, are located. At the station of La Tuna, my former traveling companion, Don Pedro, the missionary of Las Cruces, will meet me in order to accompany me to the Sacramento Mountains.

At Mass, with a few heartfelt words I encourage the fine people of Anthony to continue the work, so well begun, on the erection of their chapel. The resources to finish it are lacking, I know.

With an eye toward coupling the example with the lesson, I search the depths of my pockets on the spot and offer them what I find there, in order to aid them in bringing their pious enterprise to a satisfactory resolution. An approving murmur testifies that I have touched a grateful chord in their hearts; and as soon as Mass ends, followed by a last confirmation ceremony, the notables of the place confer, in order to discuss a means for completing the construction that is so desired.

In the earth home where breakfast was served, the table disappears under the bouquets of roses of Castile, a half-wild species that grows easily in the region. There is not a child who does not come to offer his bouquet of flowers. But time is pressing. Quickly, I jump in the wagon. Father L. straddles his faithful mount; and then we are departing for the station, located in the middle of the brushwood, above the valley. Wagons and horsemen provide an escort.

Before boarding the train, there is a new avalanche of roses of Castile, and then the farewells, touching farewells, which prolong themselves until the moment when the train gets underway and carries me off.

XIII

El Paso. Ciudad Juárez. Tularosa.

Soon the station of La Tuna is out of sight. For some time the valiant Father L. gallops superbly along the iron track; the train little by little draws away from him, moving toward El Paso. But on the stroke of noon, at the hour of dinner, Father L. is there, fresh and fit, as if nothing is unusual, having covered in one breath the distance of thirty-four to thirty-five kilometers.

Don Pedro, faithful to the rendezvous, is on the train. We arrive together in El Paso and go immediately to the residence of the Jesuit Fathers, who from this center penetrate into Texas, New Mexico, and Chihuahua. This mission is served by the PP [sic] Jesuits of the Province of Naples. The priests, almost all Italians, receive us with open arms according to their custom.[56] It is here that, after having been cut off so long from news of the civilized world, we learn, from the newspapers, about the dreadful catastrophe in Martinique and, at the same time, the death of the greatly venerated and beloved Archbishop of New York, Monsignor Corrigan.[57]

The PP Jesuits here serve two churches, one for the Americans, the other for the Mexicans. El Paso, born but yesterday, is today a city of 25,000 souls. And the population goes on growing every day. Located on the Mexican-American border, the city is the most important port of entry between Mexico and the United

States for the products of these two countries. A half dozen great railroad companies in the eastern states have their terminus in El Paso, on the doorstep of the deserts of Arizona. Hierarchically, El Paso is part of the Diocese of Dallas.

The bed of the Rio Grande separates the United States from Mexico. An international bridge unites the two cities of El Paso, in America, and Ciudad Juárez, in Mexico. The latter has eight to ten thousand inhabitants. It is the head of the line of the *Central Mexicano*, which goes deep into the south, as far as the capital of Mexico, a distance of 1,965 kilometers. This railroad company was founded and is run by American capital.

I know of no contrast more striking between two different civilizations than that which exists between these two border cities. In the time required to cross a bridge, the traveler leaving El Paso falls into the middle of Latin America in Ciudad Juárez. On one side English—the Anglo-Saxon: feverish animation, a point-to-point race in the pursuit of business and profit, a mass of utilitarian buildings, graceless, without concern for charm; on the other bank of the river, a small, peaceful city with low houses, cut by narrow streets, decorated by a plaza planted with trees where idlers come to dream in the shade, and provided with costly municipal buildings of a European appearance.

Ciudad Juárez, the westernmost city in Mexico, is also the oldest city in this region. It was founded as a mission center by the Spanish in the middle of the seventeenth century. Its church, which dominates the city from the top of a hill, is built like a fort, with walls of an enormous thickness and a few small windows which leave the interior in a half darkness, cool and conducive to meditation. Statues in the Spanish taste, dressed from head to foot in silks of bright colors, trimmed with laces and ribbons, decorate the altars.

The valley of the Rio Grande below Ciudad Juárez was previously rich and prosperous. For a number of years, because of a lack of water, cultivation has had to be abandoned, and the countryside presents a desolate aspect.[58] The mountains which border the horizon offer no sign of vegetation. Rains are rare; chronic drought reigns. All this region, in sum, is not very attractive. On the American side, the prosaicness of existence and of all things, with this horrible struggle for life which vilifies everything; on the Mexican bank, the aridness, the inactivity, the depression. And to say that these are the large cities of the Southwest! With its 25,000 souls, El Paso by itself has double the population of any other city in its diocese. Tucson, the episcopal residence, counts scarcely seven to eight thousand inhabitants. It is true that the desert that surrounds it would have trouble nourishing more.[59]

At 8:00 in the evening, Don Pedro and I are at the Rock Island station. The train that is to take us to Tularosa leaves an hour late. It loses more time en route, in the middle of the brushland, in a black night, where nothing can be discerned but vast, gloomy solitudes. Moreover, there are very few travelers. Across from me a tall American, already aging, suddenly throws all the train into an uproar by crying "Fire!" He shakes off his coat and stamps on the coattails in terror. I hurry to help him. Fire, smoke, are nowhere to be seen. The good man believes nothing of this, cries out louder, and calls upon me, with menacing gestures, to extinguish the fire which burns his clothing. I go to all the trouble in the world to calm him, by showing him that he is the victim of an illusion. The conductor of the train, rushing up at the first cry, signals me by the wink of an eye that the poor man is deranged.

Here is yet one more soul that this infamous "struggle for life" has spoiled! In this grueling life where so many people are consumed, why should it be astonishing that, at a given moment of excessive tension, the brain explodes? This jaded world needs the safety valve that the Christian concept of life gives: moderation, this cardinal virtue of temperance, which is the regulating balance of human existence and whose cult has so small a place within the Yankee soul.

The reputation that the Americans have of doing everything in a rush finds itself scarcely justified this night in that which concerns us: the train is almost three hours late. It is 2:00 in the morning on Sunday, May 11, when it stops at the station of Tularosa. To reach this village it has been necessary for me, upon leaving Anthony, my last stop, to cross exactly 180 kilometers. We are, assuredly, in a country of great distances.

Broken by fatigue, dying from lack of sleep, I wish for only one thing: to debark incognito at Tularosa and reach some bunkbed or another in double-quick time.

This consolation is not afforded me. Despite the advanced hour of the night, the fine inhabitants of Tularosa, too, want their triumphant reception; they do not let me off. On horseback, in wagon, they are there, massed around the little station, and it is necessary, by the light of two or three lanterns, to go through all the ceremonies of a solemn entrance.

I climb in a wagon, the escort forms, and we go off in the dark night toward the village, several kilometers distant.

We advance cautiously. There, from very far off, great streams of light detach themselves from the dark, obscure void. This is an illumination which outlines the contour of the church and of the adjoining rectory, giving them grandiose proportions. Soon the bell sounds loud and clear; firecrackers explode, frightening our horses, which swerve alarmingly at each detonation. It is necessary to send a dispatch rider to stop the cannonade. We cross ditches filled with water. Finally, here we are at the door of the church: arrival ceremony before the altar, then presentation of the notables of the parish, etc., etc. Finally, I am alone in the chamber which has been assigned to me. It is time; I was about to collapse from fatigue.

The next day, or rather that same day, after a restoring sleep, I celebrate the sacred mysteries before a large audience of Mexicans and address the sermon to them. Confirmation follows. Then a rapid inspection of the surroundings, for as soon as dinner is taken it is necessary to leave again by wagon in order to reach the village of Alamogordo in the afternoon, confirmation there having been announced for 4:00.

XIV

Departure from Tularosa and arrival at Alamogordo. End of pastoral tour. Embarkment on a freight train.

The village of Tularosa is an oasis in the desert.[60] Built at the foot of the Sacramento Mountains, it is bathed by the waters of springs descending from the heights. A square mile in area, it is a checkerboard of small enclosures, each containing its small adobe home and its orchard beside small working fields where grains are produced in abundance. It is noteworthy that in all the regions recently crossed in the course of this trip, no cultivation of tubers is observed. The potato, for example, is never found.

The bean, or *frijol*, the main dish on the Mexican table and, in fact, the national food, plays the same role here as the potato does in Europe. The Mexicans of our lands do not cultivate the latter because, as one has assured me, the soil refuses to produce it. The *patate*, when it figures on the menu, results from imports from the United States.

In the fortunate village of Tularosa, it is a pleasure to see the fresh waters of the mountain flow to fill the banks of the irrigation canals. The altitude, which exceeds 4,000 feet, moderates the heat of the day; the nights are deliciously fresh and serene.

We climb to the flat roof of the church. On the edges, the stubs of candles which served as illumination are still aligned, planted in sand in the bottom of paper sacks.[61] From this elevated point, the eye embraces all the oasis, which spreads out like a great garden between the mountain and the desert. The latter begins brusquely, in all its wild nakedness, without any transition, at the edges of the village, of the paradise of greenery that is Tularosa. No doubt the waters from the mountain, completely absorbed by the plantings there, do not go beyond the village limits.

In the distance, in the middle of the sands, the train station, so animated the night before, appears all alone, small and lost in the deserted immensity. Only twice every twenty-four hours a train of travelers makes a stop here, bringing a little life for several instants. Then silence reestablishes itself around it, and it falls asleep again in its solitude. This isolation, however, is not absolutely sad, thanks to the bursting sun which never ceases to shine brightly from morning to evening every day of the year.

Sixteen miles from Tularosa, in the mountains, lives the Indian tribe of the Mescalero Apaches. It would be a matter of building a small mission chapel here, the Indians showing themselves to be admirably disposed to this, but the funds are lacking with which to do it.

> In the service of Austria,
> The military is not rich,

as the song says. We must wait for the Dispenser of all good to send us the necessary resources by the means known to Him.

In the afternoon we climb into the vehicle that will take us to Alamogordo.[62]

Since we do not yet have a chapel in this village, it has been decided that the confirmation will take place in a house in the Mexican quarter.

Arriving at the site, we find a large assemblage of people, several of whom have come from very far, who have been awaiting us for hours. We have all this congregation enter into a large room which constitutes the entire house and at the end of which a table stands, covered with white linens by way of an altar. We are not slow in ascertaining that the room is too small for the crowd, which grows larger at each instant. The people are literally crushed. There is only one solution: to go outdoors and administer the confirmation in the open air.

While the missionaries accompanying me are having young and old form two lines and putting some order into the confusion, I look for a corner away from the crowd where I can take off my traveling clothes and put on the pontifical ornaments.

At the end of the courtyard, there is a wooden building to which I take my suitcase and do my business. This is a kind of kitchen, three or four meters square and crowded with a thousand things: I have trouble turning around in the midst of chickens, cats, dogs, which live happily together in this retreat and consider me an intruder.

The violet cassock is not to the dogs' taste. I have scarcely put it on when they become enraged, advancing toward me showing their teeth. I have just time to slip nimbly outside, to avoid a catastrophe.

Everything is ready. In full sunshine, under the blue dome of the firmament, in the great temple of nature, the rites of the sacrament are accomplished in good order, under the astonished but respectful eyes of a group of American Protestants attracted here by curiosity. Some hundred children receive confirmation. The ceremony complete, all this group disperses, calm and happy, godfathers and godmothers exchanging emotional embraces and going off to celebrate, by domestic merry-making, the memorable event of the day.

At Alamogordo my pastoral tour comes to its end.

There remains only to think about the return. I am 633 kilometers from my Tucson residence. The sole way of returning home is to go to El Paso in order to take there the Southern Pacific train coming from New Orleans, with a destination of San Francisco via Southern Arizona, where Tucson is located.

To reach El Paso, I have available to me the Rock Island line. But 186 miles north of Alamorgodo an accident has occurred—a bridge has burned—and train traffic has been suspended. Crossing the 128 kilometers of desert that separate me from El Paso by wagon is out of the question. It is obviously better to wait; up there, in the north, the Americans will quickly establish a provisional passage in place of the destroyed bridge, and a train en route to the South will soon appear.

We are resigned to the wait, Don Pedro and I, and we decide to console ourselves with a comfortable supper when, wandering around the train station, we learn that a special freight train formed at Alamogordo will leave at 8:00 in the evening, going to El Paso. We are granted the privilege of a place on board, if we wish, since there is no passenger train. What a windfall! Alas! We are ignorant of the tribulations that await us. . . .

At precisely 8:00, armed with our complimentary tickets, and carrying our baggage, we are at the train station, moving across the tracks in search of the train that is about to depart. Wagon 523 has been assigned to us. The night, which falls quickly in these latitudes, is already black. In the meleé of tracks and countertracks, all loaded with cars and entire trains at rest in the freightyards, it is impossible to discern this wagon 523. No noise, no locomotive smoke in sight. And not a living soul from whom to obtain information!

Finally, after many comings and goings, we glimpse, far off and all alone, a train that is almost lost in the darkness. We hurry. On the last wagon, in dirty white on a background of soot, stands out the coveted number: 523! Our car!

I have had many previous occasions in hurried visits to the sick over great distances, to travel, by special permission, on freight trains. These are generally provided at the end with a closed car known as a caboose. It is here that the crew of the train stays—the conductor and the brakeman. Equipment to forge replacement parts and everything that would be necessary in case of accident is collected here. It is hardly a comfortable place of habitation, but at least one finds a place to sit and relative cleanliness.

The infamous car 523 is not even a caboose. It is simply a boxcar, "eight horses long, thirty-two men." Not a seat, not a light, other than an infamous lantern. Dirty lubricating oil high, low, and everywhere. And not the slightest opening for ventilation except for the two sliding side doors. Since the doorstep of the car is very high, it is necessary, in order to climb it, to call upon all our old memories of gymnastics.

Once inside, Don Pedro and I look at each other in the obscurity and burst into laughter. It is decided on the spot that, out of respect for episcopal decorum, all precautions will be taken so that none of the crew will know who I am. But really, what does it matter: one must take things as they come.

Having groped around and discovered two small empty cases in a corner, we carry them to the middle and steady them as best we can; we settle ourselves there.

Suddenly, without warning, the train pulls out. With the violent and unexpected jolt, my poor companion, losing his balance, goes flying, and lands stretched out full length at the other end of the car. Since he is already aging, I fear a misfortune; I rush and help him to pick himself up. No harm. We're off! So much the better! Alas! *Initium dolorum.*

XV

Tribulations of a traveler in a freight car. La Jarilla. From El Paso to Tucson. Drought.

It is around 9:00 in the evening. Decidedly, we now are leaving for good. It is impossible to doubt, moreover, the shocks, countershocks, violent jolts, and irresistible collisions which punish us. Clinging like grim death to our cases, we force ourselves to present a good face to the world.

There are two men with us in this large box, well-named boxcar in English: the conductor of the train and the brakeman. They study us without saying a word. They have their sea-legs. But I firmly believe that I surprise them laughing up their sleeves. And, frankly, there is reason. At every moment, our cases teeter under us. It is impossible, moreover, to hold oneself erect. When, as we are descending, the end-on collisions call a truce, then there are vertical jolts because of the brakes, an abominable agitation worse than all the rest, as if the train were rolling on cogwheel tracks. These jolts, repeated a thousand times a minute, are extremely disagreeable. They shake us frightfully, from feet to head, and the torture seems interminable.

To complete our distress, the conductor estimates that we will be lucky if we can arrive in El Paso around 1:00 in the afternoon. Sixteen hours to go 138 kilometers, and under these conditions! This is not pleasant! Don Pedro begins to feel sick, and complains of nausea. For a moment the idea occurs to me to ask the conductor to stop and put us on the ground. But what would we do there, all alone in the middle of the night in the midst of the desert? This is not practical. It is necessary to resign oneself to the inevitable. But then, whatever are we doing here? Do we not know that the railroad of the Far West is the epitome of primitive? The tracks were built as they went along; the box cars were constructed without ballast, which is absolutely unknown; the regular passenger cars would be just like our box car, instruments of torture, were it not for the highly perfected system of superimposed springs, complicated buffers, elastic seating, and padding in all the upholstery with which they are armed.

Don Pedro endures no longer; he is sick. He goes to stretch his entire length against the wall of the car. . . .

As for me, I have held up well until now. How much longer will this go on? Minutes seem like hours. The air is thick, suffocating, saturated with dust. The crewmen look at me out of the corners of their eyes. Out of self-respect, I straighten up, playing the brave one. But the battle is too unequal. At the end of an hour or two, I have to knuckle under and, jostling boxes and suitcases, I go to join my companion at the back of the car, in a horizontal position. This is what saves us. The kind of seasickness which has seized us calms little by little, and our fatigue is such that soon, losing our consciousness of the situation, we are snoring, sleeping like logs.

A ray of daylight is filtering into our rolling prison when I awake. The train is not moving. I push open one of the sliding doors. It is broad daylight outside. The sun is rising joyfully; the morning air is fresh and delicious. I jump to the ground; Don Pedro is not slow in following me. Our crewmen have disappeared. Several hundred meters away a station can be seen. This is La Jarilla.[63]

From 9:00 in the evening to 5:00 in the morning, we have traveled fifty-nine kilometers. There remain seventy-nine for us to cross in order to reach El Paso. At this pace, surely, we will not arrive before evening.

No other house in sight except for the little station. In all directions, there is brushland as far as can be seen, with a horizon of mountains in the far distance. We make the hundred steps in order to stretch our muscles. Life is made up of contrasts: at that moment, there are not two happier men in the world; we survey the firm earth joyously, sucking in the delights of the pure air of the desert, and forgetting the pitiful state of the dirtiness of our clothing, or, rather, having no remedy for this.

The train's stop prolongs itself indefinitely. We go for information. At this precise moment, the conductor comes to advise us, with a big smile, that our torture is coming to an end: the station has been informed by telegraph that a passenger train, coming from the North, is descending at top speed toward El Paso. In fact, a quarter of an hour later, the freight train having been hastily removed from its path, a superb convoy descends toward us at great speed. It consents to stop to take us on.

Two hours later, Don Pedro, overjoyed, sights the silhouette of the Organ Mountains, at the foot of which Las Cruces is located. El Paso is easily imagined to the south, at the end of the valley.

Several more minutes of journeying at full steam, and then we sight the dry bed of the Rio Grande separating the modern city of El Paso, with its smoke, drab buildings, and dust, from the ancient pueblo of Ciudad Juárez, drowsy, asleep in its profound peace. On the elevated slope that we are descending, we rise over all the old Spanish city. White under the bursting sun, it scatters its low houses with windows garnished with wrought-iron bars; one sees that the interior courts, or patios, are in Andalusian style, decorated with flowers and greenery around the fountains, recalling the courtyards of the old monasteries. Above the narrow streets, the old church rises on its knoll, watching over the peaceful city . . . we arrive.

Ashamed of our appearance, barely presentable, we reach, by the shortest path, the always hospitable house of the good Italian Jesuit Fathers. There we perform our *toilette* at length. Then, the hour comes; I separate myself from my hosts, from my faithful traveling companion Don Pedro, who is returning to Las Cruces, and I go to meet the Southern Pacific train which is to take me to Tucson, 495 kilometers to the West.

The boredom of this crossing, in itself very monotonous and highly painful, is eased considerably by the agreeable company of three Spanish priests whom I meet on the train.

They are coming from Guanajuato (Mexico) and are going to California in order to give parish missions. I amuse myself by soliciting their impressions of the view of the wild solitudes which we are traversing, and which have long been familiar to me.

"*Cómo le gusta este país?*" [How does this land strike you?] I ask one of them.

"*Horro-ro-so!*" he says, "*Horro-ro-so!*"

Nevertheless, scattered in these vast deserts of the South, that give at first view the impression of repulsive ugliness, there are souls; and in this arid field, the Father of the family has workers, faithful servants who have renounced the joys of the motherland and pursue bravely, in the hope of eternal reward, their jobs as missionaries.

Upon my return to my episcopal city, I find the population of Tucson extremely afflicted by the persistent drought. For eight long months not a drop of water has fallen. The alkaline soil, cracked and split, has the hardness of cement, and on its lime whiteness the sun is reflected with a brightness that is painful to the eye. The maximum temperature in the shade oscillates for weeks between forty and forty-five degrees centigrade. Sometimes a wind comes up, the sirocco, simoom, or khamsin, which burns everything in sight with its fiery breath. Upon contact, trees lose their foliage; flowers dry up without blooming; plants die. With what close attention one watches for the apparition of the least cloud in hope of an approaching rain. Alas! *Nubes sin aqua.*

The old Indian sagamores affirm that in olden times the sky of Arizona was less implacable, the rains less rare, the climate more gentle, the earth more generous. And they blame the "pale faces" for this disastrous change. The old sagamores are wise ones; they are sometimes mistaken, but often they see the truth.

Notes

1. Bishop Granjon's series entitled "Le Long Du Rio Grande—Souvenirs D'Une Visite Pastorale" appeared in the 1903 (Volume 35) issues of *Les Missions Catholiques*. The series ran for eighteen consecutive weeks, from April 24 through August 21. Approximately eighteen photographs ran with the original article, but it appeared that most were scenes of what we know today as the state of Arizona. In a letter dated June 16, 1902 to the Society for the Propagation of Faith, Granjon writes, "I am finding it difficult to find some photos to accompany the narration." It appears that the photographs Granjon ended up using had little to do with the actual text. Granjon's narrative might be unknown to present-day readers had it not been for a series of interesting circumstances. Father Jean Grange, a French priest assigned to Mesilla and a good friend of Granjon's, acquired the articles and had them bound as one narrative. Grange eventually moved his rectory to property on the west side of the Mesilla plaza. Following his death in 1936, the property was inherited by Perla Alidib, Grange's former housekeeper, who had found sanctuary in the rectory after fleeing the Mexican Revolution. Alidib later sold the property to Paul and Mary Taylor, my parents, in 1952. After moving to the old rectory, the Taylors found boxes of old possessions that had once belonged to Father Grange, among them the bound journal of Granjon. It remained in storage for thirty years until Mary Taylor came across it again. She had a small part of it translated, knowing that it contained information on the history of Mesilla, which she had been researching thoroughly over the years. After reading the translation, I was so impressed with Granjon's

literary style and social commentaries that I asked Mary de López, a good friend of the family, to translate the narrative in its entirety. Within a few months she had completed the work with enthusiasm and thoroughness. Suddenly, we realized that we had in our hands a social history of the Mesilla Valley that should be shared with the public.

2. Father Ramón Ortiz was the Mexican land commissioner instrumental in bringing the earliest colonists up from the El Paso del Norte area to settle in Mesilla. He also encouraged families from northern New Mexico to settle in the same area, some of whom took up his offer.

3. Granjon's biographical information was compiled from records of the Diocese of Tucson; the Catholic Archives of Texas; the Theology Library, Catholic University of America; the University Archives, Notre Dame; and an article written in 1972 by Francis J. Fox, S. J., who at that time was archivist for the Diocese of Tucson.

4. A mestizo is defined in the Southwest as a person with mixed Spanish and Indian blood.

5. A *jacal* is a structure of vertical wood poles daubed with mud and roofed with timber and mud.

6. This is the introduction written by the editors of *Les Missions Catholiques* as it originally appeared in 1903.

7. These sub-headings, and others that appear throughout the narrative, were originally written by Granjon, or possibly by the editor of *Les Missions Catholiques*, to provide the reader with an idea of the content of the accompanying weekly article.

8. The Latin botanical terms appear as they did in the original French publication. Ten other phrases, most in Latin, that appear periodically through the text, are translated here with their corresponding page numbers.

    p. 18   illustrissima adstantium corona: most illustrious crown.

    p. 25   terra deserta, et invia, et inaquosa: deserted land, impassable and without water.

    p. 55   sui generis: one of its own kind; unique.

    p. 58   Major pars trahit ad se minorem: the greater part draws toward itself the lesser part.

    p. 94   forma facti gregis ex animo: form made of the flock, from the beast.

    p. 95   enfants terribles: naughty children.

Notes to pages 18–25

p. 101 Ad te clamamus exules . . . Ad te suspiramus, gementes et flentes, in hac lacrymarum valle: to you do we cry (we as exiled ones), to you do we sigh, weeping and mourning in this valley of tears. . . . (Translations by Gerald Brummell.)

9. Bishop Granjon's classical education, and his interest in languages, are illustrated by his use of English, Spanish, and Latin phrases throughout the original French narrative. He seems to draw upon whichever language is most appropriate for maintaining the tone and cultural background of his topic. In the narrative, words in quotations are word-for-word translations of French terms from the original. As an example, les Peaux-Rouges appears in the text as "Redskins."

10. The Southern Pacific Railroad was built to connect California with the Gulf of Mexico. Construction began east from Yuma, Arizona in November of 1878, arriving in El Paso on May 19, 1881. On March 8, 1881, the Atchison, Topeka, and Santa Fe line from Albuquerque connected with the Southern Pacific in Deming. At about the same time, the ATSF line extended a branch from Rincón to El Paso. John P. Wilson, "Historical Profile of Southwestern New Mexico," Las Cruces, NM: New Mexico State University, Cultural Resources Management Division, Report No. 21, 1975, p. 89.

11. Occasionally in the narrative Granjon refers to New Mexico as Arizona. The present boundaries of Arizona and New Mexico were established in 1863. However, since southern New Mexico was within the Diocese of Tucson, Arizona at the time of Granjon's visitation, he casually refers to the whole area covered by his diocese as "Arizona."

12. The founding of Lordsburg was the result of the construction of the railroad in 1881. The town quickly grew and prospered because of extensive mining activities being conducted in the immediate vicinity. "New Mexico Historical Records Survey," Hidalgo County, No. 12, p. 11.

13. "Redskins" was translated literally from the French original "les Peaux-Rouges." In other parts of the narrative Granjon refers to "Indians," a term he uses to describe those whom he considers the more settled and less "savage" indigenous inhabitants of the region. He also occasionally uses terms such as "squaw," which also is considered derogatory today.

14. This is a good analogy between the mirages of the desert and

the mirages of life, an example of the good Bishop's religious convictions and philosophy that he alludes to throughout the text. Granjon was not the first to write about these apparitions in the desert. Colonel Phillip St. George Cook, during his journey with the Mormon Battalion in 1846, made the following observations of mirages whle traveling through Hidalgo County in the same general area as Granjon:

> Next morning the march began before sunrise. All admired the singular and unusual beauty which followed its rising; but once or twice before had a mirage been observed. A distant mountain range became the shore of a luminous lake, in which nearer mountains or hills showed as a vast city—castles, churches, spires! even masts and sails of shipping could be seen by some.
> We came in sight of what was apparently a river, but we believed it to be sand. For hours I rode on, approaching it obliquely, but seemed to get no nearer. At last I struck it after sundown, and found it something extraordinary; it was said to be the bottom of a long dry lake or swamps. It appeared, in the obscurity, something between smooth marble and a great sheet of ice, wagons moved with traces unstretched, and made no track. "New Mexico Historical Records Survey," Hidalgo County, No. 12.

15. The sand storms of which Granjon speaks are most frequent and intense during early spring. Southern New Mexico has become infamous for these sudden storms; this has probably helped to keep the population growth rate down in this part of the state. A very impressive dust storm was televised nationally in March, 1982, when the space shuttle Columbia, scheduled to land in the Tularosa Basin near Las Cruces, had to delay the landing because of almost zero visibility in the storm.

16. In the 1970s a movie entitled "Hawmps" was made of this ambitious and hilarious project. According to local tradition, General Douglas McArthur had a close encounter with these same camels. While still a lad at Fort Selden (seventeen miles north of Las Cruces), where his father was commander in the 1880s, he was allegedly frightened by one of the surviving camels while playing on the outskirts of the fort. The entire garrison rushed out thinking that he had been attacked by Indians, only to find him staring at the hairy beast. For more information regarding the camel corps and an extensive bibli-

ography, refer to Odie B. Faulk, *The U.S. Camel Corps: An Army Experiment* (New York: Oxford University Press, 1976).

17. Deming was founded in November 1881 as a result of the westward railroad expansion. The town soon swelled in population owing in large part to the building of the railroad junctures of the Southern Pacific and Atchison, Topeka and Santa Fe lines. In 1901, Deming with a population of 2,000 became the Luna County Seat. "New Mexico Historical Records Survey," Luna County, No. 15.

18. Granjon is referring to the Mimbres River, which supported the Mimbres Indians of the prehistoric Mogollon group from *ca.* A.D. 300 to *ca.* A.D. 1250. The Mimbreños are widely known for having produced some of the most superbly designed pottery in the world. Unfortunately, the majority of the Mimbres sites have been destroyed by "pot hunters." Mysteriously, the Mimbreños had abandoned the valley and its tributaries by A.D. 1300. During the late Spanish period and throughout the Mexican period there was considerable mining activity at the copper mine of Santa Rita del Cobre, not far from the headwaters of the river. However, it was not until the 1880s that the Mimbres Valley saw an influx of Euroamerican settlers. These settlers provided the miners at Santa Rita with necessary food supplies and draft animals. Russell E. Clemons, Paige W. Christian, and H. L. James, *Southwestern New Mexico: Scenic Trips of the Geologic Past*, No. 10 (Socorro: New Mexico Bureau of Mines & Mineral Resources, 1980), p. 43.

19. Rincón was also known as Thorn Post Office back in the late 1800s when the railroad was first constructed. It is the point where the Atchison, Topeka and Santa Fe railroad, which connects with Deming, takes off on a spur to El Paso through Las Cruces. The necessity of changing trains at this point eventually caused Rincón to provide an ample supply of hotel rooms, including a Fred Harvey House that was famous for its restaurant and its excellent lodging facilities. Lenore Dils, *Horny Toad Man* (El Paso, Texas: Boots and Saddle Press, 1966), p. 69.

20. Tonuco, also known as San Diego, is the name of a prominent volcanic bluff rising high above the river about twenty-five miles north of Las Cruces. In the vicinity of Tonuco was a *paraje*, or camping place, on the Camino Real during the Spanish and Mexican periods. This *paraje* was used many times as the last stop before the ninety-mile crossing of the dreaded Jornada del Muerto [the Journey of the Dead

Man] going north, or the first camping place on the river traveling south after crossing the Jornada. Tonuco became a small station on the railroad after its construction in 1881.

Doña Ana is the oldest village in the Mesilla Valley, having been settled in the early 1840s by farmers from the El Paso del Norte area. When the county of Doña Ana was formed in 1851, the village of the same name became the county seat. American Army Dragoons were stationed here intermittently until the construction of Fort Fillmore south of Las Cruces in 1851, so that almost from its beginnings Doña Ana had a very eclectic population. By the 1860s, Las Cruces and Mesilla had achieved more importance as trade centers, and as a result Doña Ana lost its status of county seat. It has remained a fairly small settlement ever since.

21. An account of Bishop Granjon's visit to Las Cruces is described in both English and Spanish in one of the Las Cruces newspapers— the *Las Cruces Citizen* (May 10, 1902, Vol. 1, No. 16). This was a bilingual newspaper, and it is interesting to note that the Spanish version of his visit is much more lengthy and joyous than the accompanying English version. This is consistent with the fact that the Spanish population was almost entirely Catholic, while the Anglo population was largely Protestant. The Spanish and English accounts, reproduced here as they originally appeared, give the reader an idea of the attitudes of the day toward religion and Hispanics:

> Grande Recepción/Llegada del Ilustre Señor Obispo Granjon, de Tucson Arizona/Todos Los Habitantes Católicos en Movimiento/Uno de los Más Felices Días Notados en Esta Población.

"El Domingo día cuatro del actual, como ya en tiempo oportuno lo habíamos anunciado, fue la llegada del Señor Obispo Granjon de Tucson, Arizona. Desde las seis de la mañana ese día todo habitante Católico estaba en movimiento. Chico y grande, porque el distinguido viajero se esperaba en el tren de las ocho acuya ahora los espaciosos de la estación estaban llenos de gente, tanto Señoras como Señores y niños, de allí, acompañaron el Señor Obispo quien venía en un carruaje acompañado de nuestro estimado Parraco

Rev. Pedro Lassaigne sentado a la izquierda de su excelencia, y el carruaje venía en medio de la enorme concurrencia toda a pie, porque dejaron la caretela y en prueba el imponente respecto anduvieron a pie desde la estación hasta la parroquia. Fue cosa muy preciosa ver los Inditos danzando adelante del carruaje de tan noble personaje. Lo más hermosa era que cada Señora llevaba un niño en los brazos y también algunos caballeros llevaban niños en los brazos y como todos estaban ya vestidos para recibir el Santo Sacramento de la confirmación, iban todos de blanco, se lucían tanto que parecían mariposas. Bien dicen que a cada uno se le llega su día, este fue el día de los niños, y sin duda uno de los más felices de su vida, y también para todos nosotros y todos los habitantes de este lugar, por haber sido honrado con tan celebre visitador.

English translation:

> Grand Reception/Arrival of the Illustrious Bishop Granjon of Tucson Arizona/All the Catholic Residents in Preparation/One of the Happiest Days Noted in this Town

Sunday, the fourth day of this month, as we had been informed well in advance, was the arrival of the Señor Bishop Granjon of Tucson, Arizona. Since six o'clock that morning every Catholic had been in preparation. The distinguished traveler arrived at eight o'clock, at which time the depot was full of people. Both large and small, women as well as men and children accompanied the Bishop from the depot; he came in a carriage with our esteemed Rev. Pedro Lassaigne sitting on his excellency's left. The carriage proceeded to the church in the middle of an enormous concourse of people all walking from the station to the church to show their respect. It was a precious thing to see the Indians dancing in front of the carriage of such a noble personage. The most beautiful sight was that each woman carried a baby in her arms, and also some men carried babies in their arms, and since all were dressed to receive the Holy Sacrament of Confirmation, they were wearing white; they shone so much that they resembled butterflies. It is said that each has his day, and this was the day of the children, without doubt one of the happiest of their lives, and also for all of us and all the residents of this town, to have been honored by such a celebrated visitor.

Here follows the brief account given in English in the same newspaper issue:

> Bishop Granjon of Tucson arrived here last week for the purpose of confirming the children in his district. He was cordially received by a large number of the Catholics of this place who met him at the depot and escorted him to the church.

22. Las Cruces was founded in 1849 at the request of villagers of Doña Ana who wished to settle closer to some of the available irrigable land in the valley. The town was a busy trade center in the 1850s, 1860s, and 1870s, but saw significant growth in 1881 when the railroad owners and politicians decided to have the rails pass through Las Cruces instead of Mesilla. This event triggered continuous growth in the town. Today Las Cruces is the second largest city in New Mexico, with a population of 52,000. *Las Cruces Historic Building Survey* (Las Cruces: City of Las Cruces, 1981).

23. Some of the Indians referred to are those whose descendants have recently petitioned the federal government to be recognized as an official Indian tribe. The religious dances that Granjon witnessed are still being observed by the village of Tortugas during celebrations commemorating the Virgin of Guadalupe on December 10, 11, and 12, and on New Year's Day. The village of Tortugas evolved between 1850 and 1900, primarily from a mixture of Piro and Manso Indians, probably with some Tiwa and Mexican Indian blood as well. Most had come up from Senecú de Súr and El Paso del Norte, present-day Juárez, Mexico. The Piro Indians previously had migrated down to the El Paso area after the Pueblo Revolt of 1680. The physical and spiritual attributes of these people that Granjon describes are still evident today in the village of Tortugas and on the east side of Las Cruces, where many of them have traditionally lived.

24. Today the natives of the Mesilla Valley continue to observe many of the traditions and customs "as before the annexation of the lands

by the American Union." *Compadrazgo* is the relationship stemming from having godchildren [*ahijados*] and being godparents [*padrinos*]; the relationship is established after taking part in the sacrament with the persons involved. In the Mesilla Valley, this relationship is sometimes stronger than blood ties; it also causes clans to be formed. Historically, in days when death might come at any moment from any direction, *padrinos* understood that they were to care for their *ahijados* in the absence of their parents as though they were their own children. This is a very strong tie, and for those not accustomed to the tradition it takes years to understand the importance of the term. The tradition of *compadrazgo* is one that is still very much honored and celebrated.

Among other traditions observed are the reenactment of Christ's birth through the theatrical presentation of "Los Pastores" at Christmas; the observance of many of the church's feast days by a solemn Mass and a subsequent fiesta with food, game booths, and dances; large gatherings after baptisms and weddings with music and the traditional foods of *cabrito*, *chile colorado*, and *pozole*; and observances during Semana Santa [Holy Week] at Mesilla, including the guarded vigil on Holy Thursday, the Way of the Cross procession around the plaza, and the Santo Entierro [Holy Burial] procession on Good Friday.

25. The original St. Geneviève's church was built of adobe in 1859. By 1887 the small church was replaced with a much larger brick church in a Gothic-French revival style. The new structure was financed by fund-raising activities initiated by Father Pierre Lassaigne (Don Pedro) and the energetic Mother Praxedes Carty, Sister Superior of the Loretto Academy. Rosemary Buchanan, *The First Hundred Years/St. Genevieve's Parish/1859-1959* (Las Cruces, New Mexico: Bronson Printing Company, 1961). In 1968 the church was torn down and the site remained an empty parking lot until 1982, at which time a three-story bank building was erected there. The razing of the church is still a very volatile subject in the Mesilla Valley, and one that arouses much nostalgia, as the church is remembered as the spiritual and social center of town.

26. Father Pierre Lassaigne was a French priest working under Bishop Lamy with the Diocese of Santa Fé as early as 1865. By 1869 he was assigned to the Diocese of Tucson, from which he served as the resident priest in Tularosa, New Mexico from January 1870 to May 1876. He was placed in Las Cruces to serve as priest for St. Genevieve's church

in 1881, after having served in the Ysleta, Texas area since 1877. Lassaigne was a very hardworking priest. The records occasionally make mention of him traveling a distance of forty miles on horseback to hear confessions, baptize, perform marriages, and say Mass. Father Lassaigne died on July 18, 1909; the tablet put up in the St. Genevieve's sanctuary stated that he was then 72 years of age. Buchanan, p. 18; C. L. Sonnichsen, *Tularosa: Last of the Frontier West* (Albuquerque: University of New Mexico Press, revised edition, 1980); Sister M. Lilliana Owens, S. L., *Carlos M. Pinto, S. J. Apostle of El Paso* (El Paso: Revista Católica Press, 1951).

27. Since he is French, Granjon is obviously and expectedly enthusiastic regarding the merits and triumphs of the French clergy in the American Southwest. He frequently mentions the good influence of the French throughout the narrative. The French priests, originally led by Lamy in the 1850s, did indeed bring much-needed education and health care to the Southwest, as well as a great many priests to serve the many outlying regions. But they also brought their own ideals and standards, which often clashed with those of the native clergy and their parishioners. For a different perspective about the historic changes that took place in the Catholic Southwest in the latter half of the nineteenth century, two works may be mentioned: *Lamy*, by Paul Horgan, describes the French clergy's merits; and *But Time and Chance: The Story of Padre Martinez of Taos*, by Fray Angélico Chavez, presents a description of the native clergy and the local morals and traditions that kept Catholicism alive through the many neglected years of jurisdiction under the faraway Diocese of Durango.

28. On January 7, 1870, five sisters of Loretto came to Las Cruces to open the convent and school which was to be called the Loretto Academy. The academy quickly evolved into a boarding school for many pupils, with a fine curriculum including an excellent music department. At the time of Granjon's visit, Albertina Riordan was the Mother Superior of the Academy. The coming of Riordan was like "the landing of the Marines" (Buchanan, p. 61). She took hold immediately, and advertised the school so well that before long there were a considerable number of pupils, including boarders. In 1900, Mother Albertina went down to Chihuahua to bring back a group of Mexican girls, swelling the enrollment even more. Loretto Academy finally closed its doors in 1944, after having served the area for seventy-four years.

The buildings on the property were razed in the early 1960s and a shopping center built in their place.

29. It is evident from the bishop's remarks that times were indeed "bad along the Rio Grande." However, in June 1902, just a month after Granjon's pastoral visit, the National Reclamation Act was passed by the United States Congress. This act enabled the farmer, through government assistance, to "reclaim" the arid and semi-arid regions of the West by irrigation. According to a 1905 promotional brochure that might have embellished the truth a bit—Charles Coulter, *Rio Grande Valley of New Mexico and Texas* (El Paso, Texas: 1905)—a wide variety of crops were being harvested. Alfalfa was the most popular, since it assured the farmer twenty-five to sixty dollars per acre for his crop the season following the sowing. Extensive orchards of apples, pears, peaches, apricots, figs, and pomegranates were also very common, as well as wheat, barley, corn, tomatoes, chile, peas, celery, onions, asparagus, sugar beets, and grapes. Whether or not there was such a lush abundance in 1902 is debatable. But we do know that there was a renewed interest in agriculture in the Mesilla Valley since by 1905 Elephant Butte, the largest storage reservoir in the country at that time, was under construction by the United States Reclamation Service about sixty miles north of Las Cruces. Upon completion of the dam in 1916, the potential existed to irrigate all the valley land.

30. The May Devotions to the Blessed Virgin are still observed every evening during the month of May in several churches throughout the Mesilla Valley. An article that appeared in *Revista Católica* on May 4, 1904 describes the May Devotions as they were practiced around the same time of Granjon's visit:

Las Flores de Mayo

En la parroquia de Santa María, compuesta, como la major parte de las parroquias de este Territorio, de varias placitas, se celebra cada año el dulce Mes de las Flores. En cada aldea se reunía la gente todas las tardes en la capilla para practicar el devoto ejercicio. Sobre un altarcito adornado con un gusto más o menos estético se levantaba una piadosa imagen de la Virgen. En torno de ella brillaban muchas luces y se veía un profusión de flores, como lilas, geranios, rosas, etc. Hombres y mujeres, niños y niñas, iban tarde tras tarde a obsequiar a nuestra dulce Madre. Rezaban juntos el santo Rosario y las letanías. Luego cantaban un cántico, si no siempre según todas las reglas de arte, al menos, con todo fervor del corazón. Y que música tan deliciosa es ésta para los oidos de Dios y de su Madre Santísima. A más de eso, días habrá en el mes de mayo, en que en cada placita se cantaba una Misa Solemne en honor de la Virgin que costeaban los piadosos aldeanos, y en el día de su fiesta patronal.

English translation:

The Flowers of May

In each parochial church dedicated to Sta Maria, as are many among the various *placitas* of the Territory, they celebrate each year the sweet Month of the Flowers. In each of these villages, the parishioners would meet every afternoon in the chapel to celebrate the devotions. Over a small altar adorned in more or less esthetic taste, they would place a beautiful image of the Virgin. Around her shone many lights, and one could see a profusion of flowers such as lilacs, geraniums, roses, etc. Men and women, boys and girls, would go day after day to pay homage to our sweet Mother. They prayed together the holy Rosary and the litanies. Then they sang a canticle, if not always following the rules of art, at least with all the fervor of the heart. And what delightful music this is for the ears of God and of His Holy Mother. What is more, on some days in the month of May and on Her feast day, in each little town a solemn Mass was sung in honor of the Virgin, the Mass being donated by the pious villagers.

31. Granjon obviously had great contempt for Protestant missionaries. They clearly did not come in "bands" and "loaded with gold." Most were as poor as the proverbial church mouse.
32. In 1862 and again in 1865 the Rio Grande flooded and changed its course from the east of Mesilla to approximately its present location.
33. Macadam is a type of asphalt-based pavement, similar to the materials used in asphalt highway construction today.
34. The Organ Mountains have been a landmark in southern New

Mexico for hundreds of years. The jagged peaks and ever-changing colors have been the subject of paintings and photographs, and they have been included in the chronicles of early Spanish explorers and settlers. In 1598, Oñate referred to them as the Sierra del Olvido, and the chronicles of Otermín's journey in 1682 refer to the mountains as *Los Órganos* [pipe organs]. In Nicolas de LaFora's text, written between 1766 and 1768, the author refers to the Sierra de los Mansos which are "commonly called Los Órganos because of irregular peaks in this chain which resemble pipes of an organ." T. M. Pearce, *New Mexico Place Names: A Geographical Dictionary* (Albuquerque: University of New Mexico Press, 1965). The Mansos referred to by LaFora were Native American inhabitants of the Mesilla Valley, mentioned by Oñate in 1598 and also by Benavides in his *Memorial* of 1630. The Organ Mountains rise to 9,118 feet above sea level, the highest elevation in the county.

35. A description of the fertility of the Mesilla Valley is found in the following excerpt from Coulter: "Some have a preference for a river of clear water instead of the turbid waters of the Rio Grande, but it must be remembered that silt which is held in solution in this water is of incalculable value to the farmer and fruit raiser. It means, not alone sufficient moisture to produce the wonderful harvest, but a constant fertilizer to enrich and keep alive the soil for generations to come. None of the lands of this Valley have been impoverished by constant use. This Rio Grande water is freighted with the very richest chemical elements, gathered from the hills and mountains—the same manner in which the fat valley of the Nile has been perpetually renewed since the days of the Pharoah" (p. 10).

36. It was not until after the treaty of Guadalupe Hidalgo in 1848 that the first settlers came to Mesilla to make it their home. Many came from Doña Ana, a village a few miles to the northeast across the river, some of them thinking at that time that the site of Mesilla was still in Mexico. Others came from the Indian and Mexican villages near El Paso del Norte to work the lands that their *patrones* had acquired, or in some cases to work their own *terrenos de labor* [individual grants]. Mesilla was a firmly established community by 1850, with 600 residents. The following year the government of Mexico formally issued the Mesilla Colony Civil Grant to include this settlement, which was in the disputed area west of the Rio Grande. In 1854 the Gadsden Treaty

legally established the narrow strip of land including Mesilla as part of the United States Territory. The town quickly became a center of commerce and transportation, and with the protection offered by Fort Fillmore, a few miles to the southwest, farming and mining activities greatly increased. Numerous stage and freight lines established offices in Mesilla, including the Butterfield Overland Mail. Some of the finest hotels and restaurants in the entire Southwest were doing a booming business in Mesilla during the 1850s through the 1870s, when it was the largest settlement between San Antonio, Texas and San Diego, California. The town also figured prominently during the Civil War, when Mesilla became the Confederate capital of the Territory of Arizona from July 1861 to July 1862. Mesilla was a lively social center for the entire region. People came from all around to attend *bailes* [dances], theatrical presentations, and political rallies. Outlaws such as Billy the Kid and Nicolás Provencio frequented the town. At the courthouse on the southeast corner of the plaza, Billy the Kid was tried and sentenced to hang in 1881. Mesilla was as wild as the West ever was. But the Mesilla that Granjon saw in 1902 was indeed only a "shadow of itself," primarily because of one important transition that was to change the face of the West: in 1881 the railroad bypassed Mesilla in favor of Las Cruces, four miles to the northeast. The county seat was then moved from Mesilla to Las Cruces, and Mesilla's importance was soon dimmed by that of its neighbor. As a result, Mesilla has experienced little growth until recently, and has now instituted zoning guidelines for new construction, thus retaining much of its nineteenth century character. A large portion of the historic villge was placed on the National Register of Historic Places in 1982.

37. The cordial referred to as *chimaga* by Granjon is probably *chimajá*, an herb described as one used for teas, as a cordial, or for debility or stomach disorders.

38. This house was built by Augustine Morin in 1875 (*Mesilla News*, July 17, 1875) and served as the rectory. Morin came from Clermont Ferrand, France, along with five other missionaries whom Bishop Salpointe had recruited in 1869. Morin served as resident priest of Mesilla from 1872, when the Holy See officially took the Mesilla Valley out of the jurisdiction of the Diocese of Durango and placed it in the Vicarate of Arizona, until 1885. The house was built in the northwest area of Mesilla known historically as the "California District," because the road

to California passed through it. This was an affluent neighborhood at the time, which became famous for its spacious Territorial style homes with impressive gardens, vineyards, and orchards. Father Jean Grange apparently lived in this house from about 1886 until 1913, at which time the church rectory was moved to the west side of the plaza. Information on Morin from Diocese of El Paso Archives, parish booklets provided by Msgr. A. James Milano, Pastor, St. Vincent de Paul Church, Silver City, NM; Sister Edward Mary Zerwekh, C. J. S., "John Baptist Salpointe, 1825–1894," *New Mexico Historical Review*, Vol. 37, No. 2 (April 1962).

39. The earliest known mention of Father Jean Grange in the Valley is in 1875, when he was listed as pastor of the La Mesa Church. Most Reverend J. B. Salpointe, D. D., *Soldiers of the Cross: Notes on the Ecclesiastical History of New Mexico, Arizona and Colorado*, 1898 (Albuquerque, NM: reprinted Calvin Horn, Publisher, Inc.). His name then appears in the St. Genevieve's church records in 1882, when he assisted Father Pierre Lassaigne for a few years. Buchanan, p. 8. Grange was then assigned to the San Albino Church in Mesilla in about 1886 and was pastor there until 1928. He died in 1936. (San Albino Church archives.) His talent as a craftsman is still visible today to the parishioners of Mesilla, for the church that he had built four years after Granjon's visit is a product of his architectural ingenuity and French background. The folk-Gothic altars, with their fleur-de-lis motifs carved by Grange, are still in use within the church. The "old ones" in Mesilla still remember him affectionately as "Father Juan," a man to be respected and loved, but not to be crossed. Personal interview with Josefina Guerra, on file in the Rio Grande Historical Collections, University Archives, New Mexico State University Library. Father Grange is buried behind the altar that he built in Mesilla.

40. The San Albino Catholic Church in Mesilla has been located on the north end of the plaza at least since 1857. Prior to the 1860s, local tradition indicates that a *jacal* structure served as the church on the south side of the plaza. The beautiful adobe church that the bishop describes (see photo) was torn down and replaced in 1906 by the brick structure that still stands today. Father Grange was responsible for its construction, and it thus reflects the French architectural influence mixed with local touches that include a mission parapet on the facade between the belfries.

41. In the San Albino parish archives, the Confirmation Book lists 276 children who were confirmed, among whom are several who still are active members of the community.

42. The adobe of which Granjon speaks is still a very viable building medium in the Mesilla Valley. An awareness also exists of the importance of historic structures to the heritage of the area. The local architecture is described in a publication by the State Historic Preservation Office and the City of Las Cruces entitled *The Las Cruces Historic Buildings Survey* (1981).

43. The "umbrella" tree is also known as the "chinaberry" tree.

44. In Spanish, the term is written *criollo*. Since *criollo* is defined regionally as a person of Spanish blood born in the New World, Granjon's use of the word is misleading. The majority of the people encountered by Granjon were mestizos.

45. The Sisters of Mercy first came to Arizona and New Mexico in 1880, when four sisters took up their residence in a house provided for them in Mesilla. They arrived through the efforts of Bishop Salpointe, the Vicar Apostolic of Arizona, and Reverend Augustin Morin, the priest of Mesilla. The first superior was Mother Josephine Brennan, who came from the Convent of Mercy, Moate, Ireland. Two of the sisters went to Ireland in 1881 to bring back more sisters to help in teaching and carrying out the work of the diocese. The two were successful in acquiring five postulants for this distant mission area of the Southwest. See Owens, *Revista Católica Press*, 1951, and Diocese of El Paso Archives, parish booklets furnished by Msgr. A. James Milano, Pastor, St. Vincent de Paul Church, Silver City, New Mexico. The school and convent that were used by the sisters were torn down long ago. They were located on the northeast corner of Calle de Santiago and Calle Picacho in Mesilla.

46. San Miguel is a small agricultural town of about 200 families located twelve miles south of Las Cruces on State Highway 28. Records of its original settlement are scarce. The village dates back to the 1850s. It was originally the Manuel Sanchez, Baca Grant area. Personal information; Mary Taylor. A man by the name of Telles who owned land in the area opened a store and a post office in San Miguel under his name. Telles appeared on maps as late as 1916, but was eventually changed to San Miguel, the patron saint of the village. Edith Donaldson, *The History of Southern Doña County* (monograph prepared for the

Notes to page 82

Bicentennial Commission of Doña Ana County, copy on file at Thomas Branigan Memorial Library, Las Cruces, New Mexico). The original mission church was built in 1880 of adobe. Three years later, Father Augustin Morin, pastor at Mesilla, blessed the church bell, and in 1886 Father Montfort, the next pastor of Mesilla, canonically erected the stations of the cross. The adobe church was torn down in 1926 and in its place was built a larger, more spacious church of vesicular basalt from the Black Mesa, a volcanic outcrop on the west mesa a mile away. *Southwest Catholic Register*, Nov. 13, 1964. In February 1983, the San Miguel church burned, and has since been rebuilt.

47. La Mesa is a farming community located fourteen miles south of Las Cruces. Of all the villages between Mesilla and El Paso, La Mesa is the one that retains most of its nineteenth century appearance. Old, contiguous adobe homes of various colors front Highway 28. A few blocks to the east is the plaza area where the same church that Granjon visited still stands. The first settlers of La Mesa probably arrived in the early 1850s, and it was formally established as a village in 1857. In 1883, when application was made for a post office, the old name of La Mesa had to be changed to Victoria since there was already a post office by the name of La Mesa in New Mexico. The name of La Mesa was restored again in 1907. Early industry in La Mesa included extensive vineyards, from which considerable wine was shipped to El Paso del Norte. *Sun News*, February 24, 1980.

48. The San José church was officially established in 1875, with Father Jean Grange as the prelate in charge. Many say that there was a church there as early as 1853, and recent dendrochronology dates from the nave's vigas indicate that they were cut in the late 1860s. Personal communication, Tom Naylor, Southwest Mission Research Center, Tucson, Arizona, 1984. The records in the San Albino church in Mesilla show that on March 30, 1878 the bell was blessed by Father Grange. The church is one of the most impressive adobe structures in the Mesilla Valley. Its walls are six feet thick at the entrance, and the vigas for the roof reportedly were cut in the Organ Mountains, hauled to the river, and floated down to La Mesa. The hand-hewn circular wooden staircase to the belfry is unique in New Mexico. Early residents speak of high, small windows in the nave of the church serving as lookouts against Apache raids. These have since been blocked up, and are not evident today. Within the last thirty years, extensive alterations

have been made in the church structure. The dirt floor has been covered, the walls and ceiling have been stuccoed, and many of the irreplaceable religious statues have been taken down and new ones put in their place. A tin roof has been built over the flat one, with a mission parapet and a new mission-style tower. The altar that Father Grange had made and that Bishop Granjon mentions has since disappeared. Information from Kathleen Davis-Mancini, "An Architectural History of San Jose Church: La Mesa, New Mexico," prepared for the Art Department, New Mexico State University, Las Cruces, 1980; Donaldson's paper; and *Southwest Catholic Register,* November 13, 1964.

49. The Spanish spellings have been retained as they appear in the original publication. A translation of the two verses reads as follows:

> Where will she go, swift and weary,
> The swallow that leaves from here?
> But if in the country you strayed
> Seeking shelter and unable to find it!
> Next to my bed I will place her nest,
> In which she can spend the season. . . .
> I too am in the lost land:
> Oh! Heaven! and unable to fly!

50. R. P. Jesuit stands for *Reverendo Padre Jesuita,* or, Reverend Father etc. Later in the text, "P.P." Jesuit appears. It is thought that P.P. is a typographical error that appeared in the original manuscript.

51. The bound journal of Bishop Granjon's narrative had "Lafon" handwritten above L. when it was found in the Taylor house. Father Granjon apparently had written Lafon's name to clarify that reference to future readers. Father Joseph Lafon was superior of the Jesuits for the El Paso area, having Smeltertown, Texas (on the west side of El Paso along the river) as the parish church. Lafon would ride horseback once a month from Smeltertown to Chamberino and Anthony to say Mass. He was instrumental in getting the women of the area to instruct their children in the Christian doctrine. Owens, p. 124; Donaldson.

52. Chamberino is a small farming village eighteen miles south of Las Cruces and just west of State Highway 28. The area was originally settled by farmers in search of better lands as "El Refugio" and Los Amoles. By 1852, Cura Ramón Ortiz, acting as Mexican Land Com-

missioner, granted *ejidos* [commons] to the more than fifty heads of family already living there. This original settlement was located east of the present Chamberino and just east of Highway 28. It was inundated by the devastating flood of 1886, that covered the low spots in the Mesilla Valley from the foothills in the east to the sandhills in the west. Most of the adobe buildings at this first site were washed away during this flood. The residents rebuilt their village on higher ground on the sandy western mesa, where the village stands today. The church of San Luis Rey de Francia was also rebuilt at the new townsite over a period of eight years. Adobes twenty-four inches wide were used in its construction, and the vigas were cut from the *bosque* in the Valley. Marguerite Taylor-Want, "The Crumbling Adobes of Chamberino," *New Mexico Historical Review,* Vol. 39, No. 3 (July 1964).

53. The tamarind is a tropical ornamental evergreen tree. It is highly unlikely that Granjon saw trees such as this in the Mesilla Valley. He is probably talking about tamarisk, a shrub common in southern New Mexico.

54. The Mesilla Valley had long been famous for its extensive vineyards and for the production of excellent wines and brandies. Perhaps the bishop's palate was spoiled by world-renowned French wines. As quoted from a 1906 promotional brochure: "The fruit which undoubtedly reaches the nearest perfection from any and all viewpoints in the Mesilla Valley is the grape. There are perhaps no finer grapes grown anywhere than are produced here. As to the varieties, we have the Muscat of Alexandria, Flame Tokay, Mission, Malaga, Seedless Sultana, and all the varieties of the California grapes. Concords, Colman, Goethe, Delaware, Black Hamburg and many others are grown." Accounts from the *Rio Grande Republican* on June 2 and June 23, 1883 state that Thomas Bull in Mesilla had 14,000 grape vines on thirty-five to forty acres. The previous year, Bull stored 5,500 gallons of wine and 1,350 gallons of grape brandy in his adobe wine vaults.

55. Anthony is located twenty miles north of El Paso, Texas on State Highway 85, having been settled as a railroad construction town. It is divided in half by a state line, with half of the town being in New Mexico and the other half in Texas. The San Isidro chapel that eventually was built by the small, devout group of Catholics mentioned by Granjon was located two and one-half miles northwest of present-day Anthony. Soon the parishioners built a more substantial church for

the growing congregation and dedicated it to Saint Anthony. *Southwest Catholic Register,* January 22, 1965.

56. The history of the Catholic church in the El Paso area goes back to 1659, when Father Francisco García y Zúñiga founded the mission of Nuestra Señora de Guadalupe del Paso del Norte in present-day Juárez. About the time of the Pueblo Revolt of 1680, along the river just south of Juárez, the villages of San Lorenzo, Senecú, Isleta, and Socorro were established for Pueblo Indians from the middle Rio Grande (the area of present-day Socorro, New Mexico). These villages were administered locally from the mission in Juárez, formerly El Paso del Norte, and by the Bishop in the faraway Diocese of Durango. The French clergy began administering this area in December 1872. Salpointe, the first Bishop of the Diocese of Tucson, appointed Father Oliverio Ruellan to administer the existing missions of Isleta, Socorro, and San Elizario as well as that of Franklin (present-day El Paso). Because of the scarcity of clerics, Salpointe asked the Society of Jesus (Jesuits) to come to the El Paso Valley and establish missions. The first Jesuits arrived in Isleta on October 14, 1881, bringing much-needed energy and manpower to the El Paso area. However, the Jesuits soon fell out of favor with the next Bishop of Tucson, Peter Bourgade, because of unfounded rumors of mismanagement, and they were ordered to leave the Mesilla Valley by November 1890. They were invited back in 1894 by the Diocese of Dallas, which had annexed the El Paso area from the Diocese of Tucson on July 13, 1892. Father Carlos M. Pinto was named Vicar General for the County of El Paso by the Diocese of Dallas, and all the Jesuit missionary activities were placed under his charge. On March 2, 1896, the Juárez parish was also placed under Pinto's charge after the death of its much-beloved pastor, Cura Ramón Ortiz, who had been a very influential character in the history of the valley since the 1840s. Granjon probably was greeted by Father Pinto and housed at the Sacred Heart rectory in El Paso, Texas. El Paso was made a diocese on April 3, 1914. See Owens.

57. On Saturday, May 10, 1902, the *New York Times* reported that 40,000 persons perished as a result of a volcanic eruption on the island of Martinique, a French possession in the Carribean. Not since the eruption at Pompeii had there been such a catastrophe.

58. The usual wet period for the Mesilla and El Paso valleys is in July, August, and September. The drought to which Granjon keeps

referring throughout the narrative was broken within two months after his visit. Records for precipitation in El Paso indicate that only 0.61 inches had fallen during the five months prior to his arrival in the valley. June, the following month, recorded only 0.01 inches of precipitation. But the records for July show a total of 3.27 inches and for August 2.85 inches. Actually, the total precipitation in El Paso during 1902 was 10.15 inches, which is above the yearly average of approximately 8 inches. Records for weather stations in northern New Mexico indicate that precipitation was low during the early part of 1902, resulting in a low runoff from the northern mountains into the valley. The El Paso area had not had a rainfall above average since 1897, when 12.41 inches were recorded. The dry spell having been broken shortly after Granjon's visit, yearly precipitation steadily increased through 1905, when 17.80 inches were recorded. Judging from past records, days of precipitation in the valley areas are few, averaging twenty-two to twenty-five from information cited in 1920. There is a yearly average of 75 percent to 80 percent sunshine in southern New Mexico. Information from a periodical entitled U.S. Department of Agriculture, Weather Bureau, Summary of the Climatological Data Herein from the Establishment of the Stations to 1920. On file at the State Engineers Office, Santa Fe, New Mexico.

59. There are now well over a million people in the metropolitan area of Ciudad Juárez and El Paso. Granjon's statement "that the desert which surrounds it would have trouble nourishing more" might seem inaccurate, since the metropolitan population of the two cities in 1902 was only about 35,000. But with the tremendous increase in population in only eighty years, the topic of water that Granjon alluded to throughout his travels has become of utmost importance in recent years. There is currently a precedent-setting water suit in the courts between the city of El Paso and the state of New Mexico regarding rights to the precious commodity.

60. In 1862, Mexican farmers along the Mesilla Valley whose homes and fields had been destroyed by the rampaging floods of the river gathered at Mesilla to form a colonizing move to the Tularosa River at the foot of the Sacramento Mountains. The town of Tularosa was officially laid out that same year, and quickly grew into a lush oasis with extensive orchards and vineyards. Attacks from the neighboring Mescalero Apaches were numerous, and did not subside until the presidential order to locate

the Indians on a reservation was acted upon in 1871. The 1870s and 1880s were decades of friction in Tularosa because of cattle rustlers and other opportunists who frequented local bars and dances, causing great resentment among the locals. The first resident priest in Tularosa was Father Peter Lassaigne, who lived here from January 1870 to May 1876. He built a good church and rectory while he was here, as well as planting fruit trees and vineyards and establishing the first school. Today Tularosa is one of the more beautiful towns of southern New Mexico, owing in large part to the preservation of many of its historic buildings and numerous tree-lined *acequias*. Sonnichsen, pp. 11-16, 301; Salpointe.

61. Granjon's description of candles planted in sand at the bottom of paper sacks and used for illumination is one of the earliest descriptions of *farolitos*, or what have come to be termed *luminarias*, in New Mexico. This tradition has become widespread during the Christmas season in the Mesilla Valley and throughout the Southwest. *Luminarias* supposedly signify the lighting of Mary's and Joseph's way to shelter in Bethlehem. In *Lamy* (p. 126), Horgan states that candles protected from the wind were lighted to outline rooflines of houses during the Christmas season in Santa Fe as early as the 1850s. *Luminarias* also appear in the photograph of the San Albino Church in this text.

62. The town of Alamogordo was surveyed and laid out in April of 1898 before the railroad tracks arrived on June 15 of the same year. Charles B. Eddy, one of the town's founders, imported 44,000 pounds of cottonwood trees to plant in an effort to beautify the town during the first years of its existence. Today the town is largely supported by business generated by nearby Holloman Air Force Base.

63. Granjon is referring to Orogrande, named for the numerous gold mines in the nearby Jarilla Mountains that were in operation around the turn of the century. At the time of the Bishop's visit, Orogrande was known as Jarilla Junction.

Selected Sources

Barrick, Nona and Mary Taylor. *The Mesilla Guard: 1851–61*. Monograph No. 51. El Paso: University of Texas at El Paso Press, 1976.
Beck, Warren A. and Ybez D. Haase. *Historical Atlas of New Mexico*. Norman: University of Oklahoma Press, 1969.
Buchanan, Rosemary. *The First Hundred Years: St. Genevieve's Parish, 1859–1959*. Las Cruces, NM: Bronson Printing Company, 1961.
Catholic Archives of Texas, Austin.
Catholic University of America, Theology Library, Washington, D.C.
Chavez, Fray Angelico. *But Time and Chance: The Story of Padre Martinez of Taos, 1793–1867*. Santa Fe: Sunstone Press, 1981.
Clemons, Russell E., Paige W. Christiansen, and H. L. James. *Southwestern New Mexico: Scenic Trips to the Geologic Past, No. 10*. Socorro, NM: Bureau of Mines and Mineral Resources, 1980.
Coulter, Charles C. *"Land of Opportunity": The Rio Grande Valley of New Mexico and Texas*. El Paso, TX: Charles C. Coulter, 1905. (Copy in collections at New Mexico State University Library, Las Cruces, New Mexico.)
Davis-Mancini, Kathleen. "An Architectural History of San José Church, La Mesa, New Mexico." Paper prepared for Art Department at New Mexico State University, Las Cruces, 1980.
Dougherty, Catherine and Robert L. Nordmeyer. "The Most Reverend Henry R. Granjon (1863–1922), in *Shepherds of the Desert* (pp. 61–75).
Dils, Lenore. *Horny Toad Man*. El Paso, TX: Boots and Saddle Press, 1966.

Diocese of El Paso Archives.
Diocese of Las Cruces, pamphlet prepared for the *Liturgy for the Solemn Erection of the Diocese of Las Cruces in New Mexico and the Installation of the First Bishop Most Reverend Ricardo Ramirez, C.S.B., D.D.*, October 18, 1982.
Diocese of Tucson Archives, Arizona.
Donaldson, Edith. "The History of Southern Doña Ana County." Monograph prepared for the Bicentennial Commission of Doña Ana County. (Copy on file at Thomas Branigan Memorial Library, Las Cruces, NM.)
Faulk, Odie B. *The U.S. Camel Corps: An Army Experiment*. New York: Oxford University Press, 1976.
Finney, Charles G. "A Sermon at Casa Grande." *Point West* (September 1963), pp. 31–34.
Horgan, Paul. *Lamy of Santa Fe*. New York: Farrar, Straus, and Giroux, 1975.
Kennedy, P. J. and Sons. *The Official Catholic Directory, Anno Domini 1982*. New York: P. J. Kennedy and Sons, 1982.
Myrick, David F. *New Mexico Railroads: An Historical Survey*. Golden: Colorado Railroad Museum, 1970.
New Mexico Historical Records Survey. *Inventory of the County Archives of Doña Ana County, No. 7*, 1940, *Inventory of the County Records of Hidalgo County, No. 12*, no date, *Inventory of the County Archives of Luna County, No. 15*, 1942. Prepared by the New Mexico Historical Records Survey, Division of Professional and Service Projects of the WPA, Albuquerque, NM.
Owens, Sister M. Lillian, S. L. *Carlos M. Pinto, S. J.: Apostle of El Paso*. El Paso, TX: Revista Católica Press, 1951..
Pearce, T. M. *New Mexico Place Names: A Geographical Dictionary*. Albuquerque: University of New Mexico Press, 1965.
Rio Grande Historical Collections, New Mexico State University Library, Las Cruces, New Mexico. Sources consulted include historic photos, pamphlets, and taped interviews.
Salpointe, Most Reverend J. B., D. D. *Soldiers of the Cross: Notes on the Ecclesiastical History of New Mexico, Arizona, and Colorado, 1898*. Albuquerque, NM: Calvin Horn, Publisher, Inc., 1967.
San Albino Church Archives, Mesilla, New Mexico.
Sisneros, Francisco and Jose H. Torres. *Nombres: Nombres de Pila en*

Nuevo Mexico/Spanish Given Names in New Mexico. Bernalillo, NM: Las Campanas Publications, 1982.

Sonnichsen, C. L. *Tularosa: Last of the Frontier West*. Albuquerque: University of New Mexico Press, 1980.

Steeb, Mary M., Michael R. Taylor, and Anthony C. Pennock. *The Las Cruces Buildings Survey*. Las Cruces, NM: City of Las Cruces, 1981.

Taylor-Want, Marguerite. "The Crumbling Adobes of Chamberino." *New Mexico Historical Review*, Vol. 39, No. 3 (July 1964): pp. 169–80.

Paul and Mary Taylor Historical Collection, private, including notes and historic photographs.

Wilson, John P. "Historical Profile of Southwestern New Mexico." Report No. 21, Bureau of Land Management, 1975.

Zerwekh, Sister Edward Mary, C. J. S. "John Baptist Salpointe, 1825–1894." *New Mexico Historical Review*, Vol. 37, No. 2 (April 1962), pp. 1–19.

Newspapers

Las Cruces Citizen, May 10, 1902, Vol. 1, No. 16.
Las Cruces Sun News, February 25, 1979.
Mesilla News, July 17, 1875.
New York Times, May 10, 1902.
Revista Católica, May 4, 1902.
Rio Grande Republican, June 2 and June 23, 1883.
Southwest Catholic Register, November 13, 1964 and January 22, 1965.

Index

acculturation, 37, 39, 58, 61, 96; missionaries comment on, 58–59, 88; as threat to Catholic faith, 11

acequias, 3, 57, 139 n 60. See also irrigation

Ad te clamanmus exilues . . . ad, 101, 121 n 8

adobe, 52, 56–57, 134 n 42, 135 n 47. See also architecture, Mexican and individual churches

air: clearness of, 50; quality of light of, 35, 51, 87

Alamogordo, New Mexico, 108, 110, 111, 140 n 62

Albuquerque, New Mexico, 29

alfalfa (medsiago sativa), 3, 43, 51, 97, 120 n 8, 129 n 29. See also Granjon, Henry, journal of: description of vegetation in

Alidib, Perla, 119–20 n 1

alluvial soil. See irrigation

Americans: characteristics of, 18, 38, 61, 105; culture of, 34, 99. See also Anglos and Granjon, Henry, cultural bias of

Angelicum University, Rome, 7

Anglos, 5, 9, 11, 19–20; acquisition of territory by, 5, 6, 9, 26, 39, 81, 139–40 n 60; ethnic bias of, 21, 124–26 n 21; religious prejudice of, 20, 124–26 n 21

Anthony, New Mexico and Texas, 5, 96, 98, 99, 102, 107, 136 n 51, 137–38 n 55; need for chapel in, 100, 103, 137–38 n 55. See also San Isidro Chapel

Apache, 27, 29–31, 135 n 48

Apache, Mescalero, 110, 139–40 n 60

apostles. See missionaries

Arabia, 27, 28, 102

architecture, Mexican, 53, 56–57, 71–77 passim, 79, 80, 105, 116, 120 n 5, 134 n 42,

145

135 n 47, 135–36 n 48; as compared to Middle East, 58
arcwood (*Maclura aurantiaca*), 50–51, 57, 120 n 8
Arizona Territory, xi, 17, 19, 21, 31, 41, 50, 121 n 11; description of, 22
Army, U.S., 9, 28, 30, 122–23 n 16, 124 n 20
Ascension, feast of, 82, 85, 90
Aztecs, 45. See also Indians

baptism, sacrament of, 38, 42
Black Mesa, 135 n 46
Bonaparte, Napolean. See Napolean Bonaparte
Bourgade, Peter (Bishop of Tucson), 7, 138 n 56
Brennan, Josephine, Mother, 134 n 45. See also Sisters of Mercy
Bull, Thomas, 137 n 54
Butterfield Overland Mail, 132 n 36

cachinas, 37. See also Indians: sacred dances of
California, 6, 27, 28, 117, 121 n 10. See also Pacific coast
California column, 6
camels, 9, 27–31, 122–23 n 16
Camino Real, 4, 49, 123–24 n 20
cañones, 44
Carty, Proxides, Mother, 127 n 25. See also Sisters of Loretto
Catholic Church, 20, 99; history of in El Paso area, 138 n 56

Chamberino, New Mexico, 92, 93, 94, 96, 98, 136 n 51, 136–37 n 52; chapel at, 95, 137 n 52
Chihuahua, Mexico, 104, 128 n 28 mentioned
Chihuahua Trail, 4
chimaga, 52, 120 n 8, 132 n 37
Civil War, U.S., 6, 132 n 36
Colorado, 6
Colorado River, 28
Columbia (space shuttle), 122 n 15
comadre. See compadrazgo
Comanches, 27
communion, sacrament of, 96, 97; first, 42
compadrazgo, 38, 40, 53–55 *passim*, 60, 79, 95, 100, 110–11, 127 n 24
compadre. See compadrazgo
Confederates, 6. See also Davis, Jefferson
confession, sacrament of, 47, 96
confirmation, sacrament of, xi, 3, 21, 32, 35–40 *passim*, 42, 52, 53–55 *passim*, 66, 79, 84–85, 90, 95, 96, 99–100, 103, 108, 110–11; names chosen at, 54–55, 134 n 41
Congress, U.S., 129 n 29
Corrigan (Archbishop of New York), 104
cottonwood (*Populus Monilifera*), 43, 80, 83, 87, 91, 101, 120 n 8, 140 n 62
criollo, 134 n 44. See also Mexican Creole

Index

Dallas, Diocese of, 105, 106, 138 n 56
Davis, Jefferson (Senator), 26–28 *passim*, 31
death, 48, 60, 63, 88–89, 96, 101. *See also* last rites
Deming, New Mexico, 21, 25, 32, 33, 121 n 10, 123 n 17
Doña Ana, New Mexico, 5, 124 n 20, 126 n 22, 131–32 n 36
Doña Ana County, xi, 7
Doña Ana railroad station, 35
Don Pancho, 96–97
Don Pedro. *See* Lassaigne, Pierre, Father
Don Perfecto, 81–82, 91
drought, 44, 56, 79, 81, 90, 98, 105–6, 117, 118, 129 n 29, 138–39 n 58
Durango, Diocese of, 6, 83, 132–33 n 38, 138 n 56

Easter, 59
Eddy, Charles B., 140 n 62. *See also* Alamogordo
Elephant Butte, New Mexico, 129 n 29. *See also* irrigation
El Paso, Texas, 15, 21, 32, 43, 102, 104–5, 106, 111, 112–16 *passim*, 121 n 10, 123 n 19, 138 n 56
El Paso, Diocese of, 7, 8, 138 n 56; separate churches in, 104
El Paso del Norte. *See* Juárez, Mexico
Elysian Fields, 24. *See also* Granjon, Henry, journal of: analogies, mythological in

English language, 38, 96
explorers, Spanish, 22, 45, 131 n 34
extreme unction, sacrament of. *See* last rites

farolitos, 109, 140 n 61
Father Jean. *See* Grange, Jean, Father
Father L. *See* Lafon, Joseph, Father
Forma facti gregis examino, 94, 120 n 8
Fort Tejon, California, 28, 29. *See also* camels
France, 17, 42, 65, 79, 82. *See also* missionaries, French; Granjon, Henry, cultural bias of
Freri, Joseph, Father, 7
frijol, 109

Gadsden Purchase, 5, 131–32 n 36. *See also* Anglos, acquisition of territory by
Gibbons J., Cardinal, 7
godfather. *See* compadrazgo
godmother. *See* compadrazgo
Golondrina, La, 87–88, 136 n 49
Grange, Jean, Father, 51, 54, 56, 63, 64, 66, 80, 81, 82, 86, 91, 92, 93, 119–20 n 1, 133 n 38, 133 n 39, 133 n 40, 135–36 n 48; description of, 52, 53
Granjon, Henry (Bishop of Tucson), xi, 15, 94, 102, 103, 107, 130 n 31; early life, 7,

121 n 9; philosophy of life of, 39–40, 50, 53, 61, 62, 64, 86, 90, 94, 99, 101, 106, 110, 111, 113–16 passim
Granjon, Henry, cultural bias of: toward Anglos, 9, 10, 11, 18, 29–30, 37, 61, 62, 83, 88, 96, 105, 106, 107, 118; toward French, 9, 42, 82, 97, 128 n 27, 137 n 54; toward Indians, 37, 121 n 13; toward Mexicans, 10, 58, 61, 81, 94, 100, 101, 103
Granjon, Henry, journal of, 3, 8, 119–20 n 1, 120 n 6, 134 n 41, 136 n 49, 136 n 51; analogies: biblical, in, 29, 36, 54, 60; analogies: mythological in, 24, 58, 101; description of climatic and weather conditions in, 24, 25, 33, 44, 51, 54, 57, 63–64, 79, 83, 86, 87, 105, 117, 118, 121–22 n 14, 122 n 15, 138–39 n 58; description of domestic animals in, 52, 84, 95, 96; description of physical conditions and terrain in, 23, 24, 43, 50, 56, 59, 63, 81, 92, 95, 109, 110, 116; description of vegetation in, 41, 43, 51, 52, 53, 57, 81, 84, 86–87, 94, 96, 97, 109, 110, 137 n 53, 137 n 54; description of wildlife in, 22–23, 34; importance of, xi, 3, 11, 119–20 n 1, 120 n 7; phrases: botanical, in, 120 n 8, 137 n 53; phrases: foreign language, in, 120–21 n 8, 121 n 9, 136 n 49; phrases: Latin, in, 120–21 n 8. See also individual phrases
Granjon, Henry, tour of Mesilla valley by, 3, 4, 6, 15, 19, 21, 32, 33, 94, 98, 102, 111, 119 n 1, 124 n 21; gifts received on, 53, 99; travel conditions on, 23, 35, 50, 51, 66, 92, 93, 97, 98, 106, 107, 111, 112–16 passim, 117, 122 n 15
Grant County, xi, 7
grapes, 41, 51, 95, 129 n 29, 137 n 54. See also vineyards
Guadalupe-Hidalgo, Treaty of, 131–32 n 36. See also Anglos, acquisition of territory by
Guanajuato, Mexico: priests from, 117
Gulf of Mexico, 43, 121 n 10. See also Rio Grande

Harvey House, 123 n 19
hidalgo, 61
Hidalgo County, 122 n 14
holy oils, 39. See also confirmation, sacrament of
Holy See, 6, 132 n 38 mentioned

Illustrissama adstantium corona, 18, 120 n 8
Indians, 5, 36, 38, 41, 52, 121 n 13, 123 n 18, 126 n 23, 138 n 56; sacred dances of,

Index

36–37, 124–26 n 21. *See also* tribe names
Initium doloram, 113, 120 n 8
International Commission, 31. *See also* Guadalupe-Hidalgo, Treaty of
Ireland, 7, 134 n 45
irrigation, 43, 44, 51, 56, 57, 86, 92, 109, 110, 129 n 29, 131 n 35, 139–40 n 60. *See also* acequias; Elephante Butte; water
Isleta del Norte, New Mexico, 5, 138 n 56
Isleta del Sur, Mexico, 5, 138 n 56

jacal, 10, 58, 120 n 5, 133 n 40. *See also* architecture, Mexican
Jacinto (mestizo), 46–48. *See also* religion
Jesuits, 8, 136 n 51, 138 n 56
Jesuits, P. P. *See* Jesuits, R. P.
Jesuits, R. P. (Reverendo Padre Jesuita), 136 n 50. *See also* Lafon, Joseph, Father
Jiménes, Cecilio, 99, 100, 101
Jornada del Muerto, 4, 123–24 n 20
Juárez (Ciudad Juárez), Mexico, 5, 105, 116, 120 n 2, 126 n 23, 138 n 56; description of, 105; in contrast to El Paso, 105. *See also* Pueblo Revolt of 1680

kachinas. *See* cachinas

Khamsin, 117, 120 n 8

Lafon, Joseph, Father, 92, 93, 94, 96, 97, 103, 104, 136 n 51
La Jarilla train station, 115, 140 n 63
La Mesa, New Mexico, 5, 66, 81, 82, 90, 92, 95, 135 n 47
La Mesa, church at, 82–83. *See also* San José Church
La Mesa, rectory at, 82, 90
La Mesilla, New Mexico, 5, 49, 66, 119–20 n 1, 124 n 20, 126 n 22, 130 n 32, 131–32 n 36, 134 n 45; as former pearl of the valley, 56, 131–32 n 36. *See also* railroads
La Mesilla, church at, 53. *See also* San Albino Church
La Mesilla Colony Civil Grant, 131–32 n 36
La Mesilla Valley, xi, 3, 9, 51, 66, 90, 120 n 2, 129 n 29, 137 n 54; cultural change in, 11, 139 n 59; description of, 43, 44, 95, 131 n 35; history of, 4, 124 n 20, 139–40 n 60
Lamy, Jean Baptiste (Bishop of Santa Fe), xi, 6–7, 41, 127 n 26. *See also* priests, French: interclerical conflict of
Las Cruces, New Mexico, 5, 15, 21, 32, 34, 35, 45, 49, 116, 117, 122 n 15, 122–23 n 16, 123 n 19, 123–24 n 20, 126 n 22; as rival of La Mesilla, 56, 131–32 n 36

Las Cruces, church at. *See* St. Genevieve Church
Las Cruces, Diocese of, 7
Lassaigne, Pierre, Father, 35, 39, 41–42, 49, 50, 102, 104, 106, 112–17 *passim*, 125 n 21, 133 n 39, 140 n 60
last rites, 60
La Tuna: railroad station at, 102, 104
López, Mary W. de, xii, 4, 120 n 1
luminarias, 109, 140 n 61
Luna County, xi, 7, 123 n 17
Lyon Missionary Society. *See* Society for the Propagation of the Faith, Lyon office

macadam, 49, 130 n 33
Major pars trahit as se minorem, 58, 120 n 8
Mansos, 4, 126 n 23 mentioned, 131 n 34
Manuel Sanchez, Baca Grant, 134 n 46
marriage, 45, 97
Martinique (French possession), 104, 138 n 57
Mass, 33, 34, 36, 37, 52, 80, 85, 90, 96, 102, 103, 107–8
Massacre of the Innocents, 39
May Devotions, 8, 45, 96, 101, 129–30 n 30
mesquite (*prosopis pubescens*), 92–93, 120 n 8
mestizo, 10, 11, 21, 38, 42, 44, 45, 46, 71, 120 n 4, 134 n 44; characteristics of claimed by Granjon, 17, 45, 59, 60, 61, 64, 80, 82, 84, 87, 91, 93, 94, 95, 98–99, 100, 101, 126 n 23. *See also* Mexican culture
mestizo culture: appreciation of by Granjon, 11, 58, 84, 86, 96, 99, 102, 105; comparison of with European culture, 17, 36, 105; effect of tradition on, 39, 45, 59, 88, 101; poverty of, 53, 56, 60, 61, 79, 81, 100, 101
Mexican-American War, 5. *See also* Guadalupe-Hidalgo, Treaty of *and* Anglos, acquisition of territory by
Mexican culture, 23, 38, 42, 44, 45, 56, 58, 60, 61, 64, 79, 82, 87, 88–89, 102, 126–27 n 24; comparison of with American culture, 58, 82, 96, 105; family structure in, 59–60; religion, role of in, 45, 59, 79, 86, 88, 99, 101, traditions of, 9, 38–39, 54, 64, 79, 91, 103, 126–27 n 24, 137 n 54, 140 n 61. *See also* architecture, Mexican *and* mestizo culture
Mimbres, valley of, 32, 123 n 18
mirage, 24, 25, 122 n 14
missionaries, Catholic: in Southwest, 17, 41, 42, 45, 49, 88, 95, 105, 132–33 n 38, 138 n 56; deference to by Mexicans, 60, 103; functions of, 33, 91, 117, 133 n 39,

Index

136 n 51, 140 n 60; longing of for homeland, 65, 117; struggles of, xi, 100, 102
Missions Catholique, Les, 4, 119–20 n 1, 120 n 6, 120 n 7
Mississippi, 41
Mohave Desert, 28
Monfort, Father, 135 n 46
Morin, Augustine, Father, 52, 132–33 n 38, 134 n 45, 135 n 46
mountains, 22, 41, 50; Organ, 3, 50, 116, 130–31 n 34, 135 n 48; Sacramento, 22, 102, 109, 110, 139–40 n 60; San Pedro, 22; San Simon, 22; Santa Catalina, 22; Santa Cruz, 22; Santa Rita, 22

Naples, Province of, 104
Napolean Bonaparte, 27
National Reclamation Act, 129 n 29. *See also* Elephant Butte
New Mexico, Territory of, 15, 17, 21, 104, 121 n 11
Nogales, Arizona, 46, 48
Nubes sin aqua, 117, 120 n 8

Organ Mountains. *See* mountains, Organ
Orogrande, 1, 15, 140 n 63. *See also* mountains, Organ
orphans, 60. *See also compadrazgo and* Mexican culture: family structure of
Ortiz, Ramon, Cura, 120 n 2, 136–37 n 52, 138 n 56

Pacific coast, 19, 24, 27, 28
Panama, Isthmus of, 28
peanut (*arachis hypogora*), 85, 120 n 8
peanut vendor, 85–86; donkey of, 85–86. *See also* Mexican culture: traditions of
Piro Indians, 5, 126 n 23
Pius XI, Pope, 8. *See also* Holy See
potato, 109
priests. *See* Jesuits; missionaries, Catholic; and priests, French
priests, French, 6, 11, 42, 45, 133 n 39; interclerical conflict of, 6, 128 n 27
Protestants, 111; conversion of, 42; missionary activities of, xii, 46, 47–48; use of term by Granjon, 10
Pueblo Revolt of 1680, 5, 126 n 23, 138 n 56

railroad, 17, 23, 32, 33, 112–16 *passim*; El Paso, as center of, 105, 111, 121 n 10, 126 n 22, 131–32 n 36; Atchison, Topeka and Santa Fe, 102, 121 n 10, 121 n 12, 123 n 17, 123 n 19; Central Mexicano, 105; Grand Express, 19; Rock Island, 102, 106, 112; Southern Pacific, 21, 111, 117, 121 n 10, 123 n 17
ramada, 80. *See also* architecture, Mexican

Ramirez, Ricardo Espinoza (Bishop), 7
Reclamation Service, U.S., 129 n 29
Redskins, 24, 31, 36, 41, 121 n 13. *See also* Indians
religion, Catholic: defection from, 45, 46–48 *passim*
Rincon, New Mexico, 32, 33, 34, 121 n 10
Rio Grande, 43–44, 51, 96, 97, 98, 105, 116, 131 n 35; floods of, 44, 49, 82, 97, 130 n 32, 137 n 52, 139–40 n 60
Riordan, Albertina, Mother, 129 n 28. *See also* Sisters of Loretto
roads, 49, 50, 51, 56, 81, 97

Sacred Heart Parish (Tombstone, Arizona), 7
sagamore, 118
St. Etienne (Loire, France), 7
St. Geneviève (church at Las Cruces), 36–37, 41, 127 n 25, 127–28 n 26, 133 n 39
Saint Isidore Chapel (at Anthony), 99, 100, 102
St. Louis, Missouri, 24
St. Mary's Seminary (Baltimore, Maryland), 7
Saint Michael: festival of, 79; statue of, 79, 80, 135 n 46
Salpointe, John Baptist (Bishop of Tucson), 7, 132–33 n 38, 134 n 45, 138 n 56
San Albino Church (at La Mesilla), 133 n 39, 133 n 40

San José Church (at La Mesa), 135–36 n 48
San Luis Rey de Francia Church (at Chamberino), 137 n 52
San Miguel, New Mexico, 5, 66, 79, 81, 134–35 n 46
San Miguel, rectory at, 87
Santa Fe, Diocese of, xi, 6. *See also* Lamy, Jean Baptiste
San Xavier del Bac, 8
Senate, U.S., 27, 28
Senecú del Sur, Mexico, 5, 126 n 23, 138 n 56
Sierra County, xi, 7
simoon, 117
sirocco, 117
Sisters of Loretto, 42, 128–29 n 28; boarding school of, 42, 127 n 25, 128–29 n 28
Sisters of Mercy, 52, 65–66, 134 n 45; school of, 52, 66, 134 n 45
sky. *See* Granjon, Henry, journal of: description of climatic and weather conditions *and* Southwest: Granjon's ambivalence toward
Society for the Propagation of the Faith: Lyon office, xi, 3, 119–20 n 1; U. office, 7
Society of Jesus. *See* Jesuits
Socorro del Sur, Mexico, 5, 138 n 56
Socorro, New Mexico, 5, 138 n 56
Sonora, Mexico, 31
Southwest: ambivalence of Granjon toward, 33, 44, 45,

Index

51, 64, 83, 87, 101, 106, 110; comparison of with Middle East, 57; description of, 19, 63, 117
Spanish culture: Moslem influence on, 9, 102
Spanish language, 9, 38, 52, 96, 102
Sui generis, 85, 120 n 8
Su illustrissima, 81
Suplican Seminaries (Paris and Issy), 7
Supply (ship), 28

Taylor, Mary, 119–20 n 1
Taylor, Michael Romero, xii
Taylor, Paul, 119–20 n 1
Telles, New Mexico, 134–35 n 46. *See also* San Miguel
Terra deserta et invia et inaquosa, 24–25, 120 n 8
Texas, 104
Tonuco, New Mexico (railroad station), 35, 123–24 n 20
Tucson, Arizona, 106, 111, 117
Tucson, Bishop of, xi, 18, 34, 99
Tucson, cathedral at, 53
Tucson, Diocese of, xi, 7, 15, 17, 49, 121 n 11, 133 n 38, 134 n 45, 138 n 56

Tularosa, New Mexico, 5, 102, 106, 107, 139–40 n 60; description of, 109; train station at, 110
Tularosa Basin, 122 n 15

Umbrella tree (*Melia Azedarach Urbraculiformis*), 57, 87, 120 n 8, 134 n 43
Union soldiers, 6
Utile dulci, 83

Victoria, New Mexico, 135 n 47. *See also* La Mesa
vineyards, 51, 95, 96, 135 n 47, 137 n 54
Washington, D.C., 59
water: as precious commodity, 9, 24, 33, 99, 126 n 22, 139 n 59. *See also* irrigation *and* drought
Wayne, C., Captain-Major, 28
wigwam Indians, 31. *See also* Indians *and* Redskins
wind. *See* Granjon, Henry, journal of: description of climatic and weather conditions *and* Granjon, Henry, tour of Mesilla Valley: travel conditions on
windmills, 33, 41